Do You Believe?
Living the Baptismal Covenant

Do You Believe?
Living the Baptismal Covenant

NANCY ANN MCLAUGHLIN

MOREHOUSE PUBLISHING

An imprint of Church Publishing Incorporated
Harrisburg

Unless otherwise noted, the Scripture quotations contained herein are from the New Revised Standard Version Bible, copyright © 1989 by the Division of Christian Education of the National Council of Churches of Christ in the U.S.A. Used by permission. All rights reserved.

Morehouse Publishing, P.O. Box 1321, Harrisburg, PA 17105
Morehouse Publishing, 445 Fifth Avenue, New York, NY 10016
Morehouse Publishing is an imprint of Church Publishing Incorporated.

Cover art:
Cover design by Laurie Klein Westhafer
Page design by Jennifer Glosser

Library of Congress Cataloging-in-Publication Data

McLaughlin, Nancy Ann.
    Do you believe? : living the baptismal covenant / Nancy Ann McLaughlin.
        p. cm.
    Includes bibliographical references (p.   ).
    ISBN-13: 978-0-8192-2192-6 (pbk.)
    1. Baptism—Reaffirmation of covenant—Episcopal Church. 2. Lay ministry—Episcopal Church. 3. Spiritual life—Episcopal Church. I. Title.
    BX5949.B2M35 2006
    283'.73—dc22
                                        2005035412

Printed in the United States of America

06 07 08 09   10 9 8 7 6 5 4 3 2 1

To John and Jason
Thomas and Stephen
all children of God

CONTENTS

LIST OF FIGURES

ACKNOWLEDGMENTS

Thank you to those individuals who responded to my request for recommendations for this study. Thanks especially to the representatives who shared their congregational and personal faith stories with me. May God bless all of you in your ongoing ministries!

Thanks to all the people who got me started on this journey.

Thanks to Lynne Wilson for her life and ministry.

Special thanks also to Liz Simmons; and St. Stephen's Episcopal Church in Phoenix, for the use of the Reverend Wil Stewart library; to the Seabury Institute staff, especially John Dally and Newland Smith; and to the staff at Morehouse Publishing, especially Nancy Fitzgerald, Ryan Masteller, and Jen Hackett.

—◦ Thanks to my writing advisor and friend Bettie Anne Doebler and to my understanding boss James Helfers.

—◦ Thanks to Thomas and Stephen.

—◦ Thanks, John ("Don't you have a paper you're supposed to be writing?")

—◦ and Jason ("I think you need a hug!").

—◦ Thank you to "all my special people who I pray for all the time."

—◦ Thanks, God, for giving me everything I need.

SECTION ONE
RELATIONSHIP WITH GOD

1549 Instructions to Godparents

Then standyng at the fonte
the priest shall speahe to the Godfathers and Godmothers, on this wyse.
Wel beloved frendes,
ye have brought these children here to bee Baptized,
ye have prayed that our Lorde Jesus Christ would vouchsafe to
receyve them,

> to lay his handes upon them,
> to blesse them,
> to release them of theyr sinnes,
> to geve them the kyngdome of heaven, and everlastying life.

Ye have heard also that our Lorde Jesus Christe hath promysed
in his gospel,

> to graunte all these thynges that ye have prayed for:
> whiche promyse he for his parte, will moste suerly
> > kepe and perfourme.

Wherfore, after this promyse made by Christe,

> these infantes muste also faythfully for theyr parte promise
> > by you, that be theyr suerties,
> that they wyll forsake the devyll and all his workes,
> and constantly beleve Gods holy woorde,
> and obediently kepe his commaundementes.

The Book of Common Prayer, 1549

1

CHAPTER 1

What Is God Asking Me to Do?

Now the word of the LORD came to me saying,

> *"Before I formed you in the womb I knew you,*
>
> *and before you were born I consecrated you;*
>
> *I appointed you a prophet to the nations."*

Then I said, "Ah, Lord GOD!

Truly I do not know how to speak, for I am only a boy."

But the Lord said to me,

> *"Do not say, 'I am only a boy';*
>
> *for you shall go to all to whom I send you.*
>
> *and you shall speak whatever I command you.*
>
> *Do not be afraid of them, for I am with you to deliver you,"*

says the LORD.

Jeremiah 1:4–8

When I was about five years old, I remember consciously deciding to be "good." Having been raised Roman Catholic, by that point I'd already heard much about God both at church—through the Sunday readings and preaching—and every day from my mom—through what she said and by her family devotional life. "Being good" was what God wanted me to do and I decided that was what I wanted, too.

Growing up in a dysfunctional family was rough, though, and I looked to the church to provide me with stability and consistency. After all, church was where they talked about a loving God and everything that was *really* important. When I was in the seventh grade, I even thought that God might be pleased if I chose to be a priest. But I was young, and being female and only knowing the Roman Catholic world, I could make little sense of me thinking that God would want me to do something that was impossible. But it did seem as though God wanted me to do *something*.

In college I was active as a religious education teacher for the fourth through sixth grades, and I observed that being a parish religious education director was apparently the slot for people like me. The year I was to graduate from college, however, there came a notice that the local major seminary was accepting applications for a scholarship program, and it wasn't limited to ordination-bound candidates. Wow! I thought, "That would be great—it would have to be a marvelous education—it's the same that they're giving their *priests* after all, so it's got to be the best." So I spent four more years in school, this time taking the same courses that the Roman Catholic priesthood candidates were taking. Not only were we in class together, we worshiped together and we shared meals together.

Upon graduation from seminary with two master's degrees, I found employment in a large Roman Catholic church as a director of religious education. I was responsible for junior high and high school programs, including confirmation preparation and retreats, as well as for programs aimed at adults, such as RCIA (Rite of Christian Initiation of Adults), Bible study, and preparation for infant baptisms. Quickly I realized that working for a church was different from the ideal I'd imagined in seminary: it was full of politics. And so after just a few years, when I said that I was interested in working more specifically with the adult programs, I was told by the pastor that his interest was moving more toward the youth programs.

After that, I worked briefly for a bank, and then a hospital system, a couple of schools, and the Census Bureau. For many years, I also had my own home-based typesetting business. I volunteered extensively at my sons' grade school: coordinating a student newspaper, chairing committees, doing book fairs, and teaching computer classes. But the only church services I attended regularly during those years were family funerals. I realized, however, that God was still there with me, and the church as an institution was waiting patiently on the back burner. So when my eldest son started high school and my time was freed from the volunteer work, I met my husband for lunch one day and told him that I decided to check out the Episcopal Church and invited him to come with me. He declined and so I went alone.

I found this church open and welcoming, no matter what I told them about myself and my background, and I began to get involved in parish activities. Once the priests and parishioners discovered my educational history, not only did they assume I wanted to be a priest, but they also started to ask me to take on more responsibilities, like working with the Alpha program or establishing small group communities. It was great to be accepted so readily! But I hadn't been involved in church stuff for years—the master's degrees were twenty years old! So I got on the Internet and surfed a bit and found a program in "Congregational Development" run out of Seabury Western Seminary that looked like it might help me get back up to speed. They accepted me and I spent several weeks for the next three summers with two dozen ordained classmates, both men and women. We shared classes and meals together and with our presenters who were key authors from several denominations. Time between the summer sessions we studied independently: reading, writing reports, and conducting research.

Now, during my first few months in the Episcopal Church, other things were also going on in my life. This was one of those transitional moments when I was consciously open to the Holy Spirit's action. I found myself reexamining *everything*. I rediscovered in a new way that Jesus is real, that God cares about me, and that the Holy Spirit is willing to assist. And I knew if that's what I really believe, then that's what I had to act on—*now*. I ended up realigning many things in my life, and I continue to reorganize as I still seek God's guidance in what is right and what is good. The initial reason for the course work no longer existed, but it seemed as though God had been letting me know that finishing this program and writing the final paper—upon which this book is based—was important.

In the following chapters we will explore Christian baptism as the covenant between God and believer. In order to do this in a tangible way, we will concentrate on the Episcopal Church. Since its inception of the 1979 version of the Book of Common Prayer, this denomination has consciously referred to its baptism ritual as "The Baptismal Covenant." And, in using this covenantal formula, this faith community urges the continuing affirmation of five specific covenantal vows concerning the realization of the Christian life (BCP, 304–305).[1] In particular, we'll look at some forty Episcopal parishes to see how they might have started to internalize this ritual covenantal agreement in their ongoing lives.

But why are these two pages of the Book of Common Prayer so important? Just what is it that I'm trying to accomplish by writing about the concept of covenant in this book? The main goal is, of course, to have people come to an awareness of some of the depth involved in being a baptized Christian, a follower of Jesus. But the issue is complicated by the church—probably most specifically in the differing perspectives of the *ordinary* Christian and the *ordained* Christian. Let me show you what I mean by telling you a story about the origin of this book and the research project on which it is based.

One summer at Seabury all the members of our doctor of ministry class met with the director to discuss what their research topic would be. I hadn't given my topic much prior thought since I had other things on my mind: staying solvent after a divorce, raising two teenage boys, and coping with a stressful work environment. But since I was the only non-ordained person in our group, I said, "Well, I suppose I could do mine on lay ministry." The Reverend John Dally, the institute director, readily agreed, mentioning that no one else in the program's history had addressed the specific topic directly before. He also mentioned that the Presiding Bishop's wife, Phoebe Griswold, had asked him recently what the Seabury Institute was doing for the laity. He also went on to say that I'd need to address the topic from the perspective of the 1979 Book of Common Prayer's baptismal covenant.

So I worked on the project between the full-time job and the single parenting, and when I submitted a partial, very rough first draft, I was reminded that I was supposed to have been doing the project from the orientation of the baptismal covenant—which I'd somehow forgotten along the way. Now I'll admit that although I'd put my heart and soul into the work I'd done up to that point, there was probably a good deal of "venting" that took place while I wrote that first very rough draft as well. And when my chairperson told me to take a wholly different approach, I'll also admit that I was at that place where many an ABD (all-but-dissertation) doctoral candidate asks, "Is it worth it?" At the time, I worked as an assistant to the dean of a liberal arts college in a Christian university, and I remember discussing with many of the professors on the hall both (1) "why *baptism*" would be the necessary link to ministry, rather than, say, being made in the "image of God," which would open the study not only to ecumenical arenas, but to inter-faith dialogue as well, and (2) "but that's a *clergy* perspective"—regular Christians, after all, typically rely on their relationship with God and the world, not specifically on their baptism, to figure out what to do. And so after thought, discussion, and prayer—and that continuing sense from the Spirit that this project was impor-tant—I went ahead and did the paper from the Episcopal baptism covenant per-spective. (After all, I reasoned, the degree would be from an Episcopal seminary, and they do have the right and duty to set their own standards.) And, if I did it right, adding my own insights, I hoped this project would be helpful in a number of ways. First, I thought, it might help open a dialogue with clergy from their own perspective. Second, I thought it might give regular Christians an educational resource for their own spiritual growth, plus a means of better understanding the clergy perspective. Third, I hoped it would be valuable to a wider faith audience by noticing our basic similarities while recognizing our differences. Finally, of course, I wanted to develop my personal patience and fortitude, and show that I, too—a mere "lay" person—could jump through the hoops that are part of getting a doctor of ministry degree.

So off I went again doing more research; to me research is *fun*. I investigated ancient Near East covenant treaties, early church baptismal rites, reformation history, other denominations' baptismal rites, and the development of the Book of Common Prayer. Then I incorporated those understandings into what was left of the first manuscript. I further evaluated the congregational interviews against the specific promises outlined in the current Episcopal baptismal covenant. I did this all while working full time, being a single parent, and dealing with my pastor, who wondered why I didn't choose to spend more time involved in "church" activities. And, when I took in two foster kids—brothers aged nine and ten—my thesis committee chairperson responded, "Now you'll never finish!" But after just another year of work, my committee accepted my work and I was scheduled for graduation. During the final oral review, however, my chairperson mentioned that the Reverend Loren Mead, founder of the Alban Institute, had written a pertinent article recently. I was shocked by what I heard; did Mead actually say, "the baptismal covenant is a bust" as the chair had seemed to indicate? Well! I'd have to track down that article!

Entitled "Lay Ministry Is at a Dead End," Loren Mead wrote: "I'm serious in saying what's unmentionable. 'Lay ministry' as a genuine goal for people in religious institutions is not a viable construct."[2] Mead explained that, although many have written and talked about the subject for years, not much has actually happened.

> Where there is that kind of consensus about something, yet nothing changes, I sense that we are coming at it from the wrong direction. We act as if another book, or another program, or another experiment, or another process will somehow do it. This is the fallacy of thinking that continues to hope that if we keep doing the same old thing, somehow we won't get the same old results.
>
> In short, we're not dealing with a problem that only resides in our thinking or our programs or processes. We are caught up in a system—an interrelated, interconnected set of relationships that reinforce homeostasis. Anything we do to enhance lay ministry causes a reaction in the system that negates what we do. The system is self-correcting. And it self-corrects back to the same old clergy-centered sense of ministry that we are trying to get away from.[3]

Hmmm. Was I coming at it from the wrong direction? Was I writing just another book or was I trying to change the system? Just what was I trying to accomplish? Well, although there's much in this book that deals with "the system," what I'd like is for individual people and congregations of Christians, with God's help, to refocus their time, efforts, and priorities on God, and on doing everything—system or no system—in response to God's love and mercy.

Loren Mead and I corresponded about these issues (and you're most welcome to write to me as well), but what really caught my attention was in his comments to me after he'd read my doctoral thesis. He said that baptism as covenant "is not . . . an idea that communicates in ordinary parishes. It's a foreign word—one used almost exclusively by clergy."[4] Oooops! Even as I thought I was writing from a lay perspective, I'd slipped into church-speak mode. It happened without my even noticing it. Remember—I wrote this while working full time as a typical, non-ordained, single mom, support-staff type person, but sometime during my "fun" research I somehow left the realm and the mindset of the typical non-ordained ("why baptism?" "why covenant?") and bought into the rich "covenant" model and its implications.

Imagine how easily that type of thing happens, on many levels, in the isolated world of seminaries. That's why I think adult education and formation are so important. This story also illustrates my qualifications for writing a book about baptismal ministry—a book that addresses both Christians and the ordained ministry as well as the church institution. My background is an interesting combination of theological education, basic (but not necessarily "churchy") Christian life ministry, and a sense of being called by the Spirit to do something important. I invite all Christians—real, ordinary ones, and those ordained for career work in the institution—to read this book. It may provide a common ground for dialogue and work on the common Christian calling—a response to Jesus' invitation: "Come follow me!"

Questions for Reflection

1. Do you have a sense of what it is that God has chosen for you since before you were born? What are you and God trying to accomplish

   with your life in general?
   with your major activities (such as work, school, raising kids, volunteering)?
   with your church community?

2. What is it that your church community is trying to accomplish with God's help?

CHAPTER 2

Covenant and Christian Baptism

The LORD brought Abram outside and said, "Look toward heaven and count the stars, if you are able to count them." Then he said to him, "So shall your descendants be." And he believed the LORD; and the LORD reckoned it to him as righteousness.

Then he said to him, "I am the LORD who brought you from Ur of the Chaldeans, to give you this land to possess." But he said, "O LORD GOD, how am I to know that I shall possess it?" He said to him, "Bring me a heifer three years old, a female goat three years old, a ram three years old, a turtledove, and a young pigeon." He brought him all these and cut them in two, laying each half over against the other; but he did not cut the birds in two. And when birds of prey came down on the carcasses, Abram drove them away.

As the sun was going down, a deep sleep fell upon Abram, and a deep and terrifying darkness descended upon him. . . .

When the sun had gone down and it was dark, a smoking fire pot and a flaming torch passed between these pieces. On that day the LORD made a covenant with Abram, saying, "To your descendants I give this land. . . ."

Genesis 15:5–12, 17–18

Q. **What is meant by a covenant with God?**
A. *A covenant is a relationship initiated by God, to which a body of people responds in faith.*
(BCP, 846)

8

Ancient Near East Covenant Treaties

In the ancient Near East, covenant treaties were often drawn up among the Amorite and Hittite peoples. The suzerainty treaty initiated by an overlord to his vassal is the type that most closely parallels the covenant forms that are used to depict the relationship between God and the Hebrew people.[1] During that time, the suzerain was the powerful lord or king of a large region. The vassals, who each lived in their own section, were expected to manage their own affairs while showing faithful allegiance and devotion to the one lord in whose kingdom they lived. If any part of the suzerain's holdings were in danger, the vassals would be called upon to come to the aid of the kingdom. Likewise, if the vassal or his extended family felt threatened, he could call upon the lord and petition for rescue. This language of lord, loyalty, and protection is reflected quite often in the Psalms.

> I say to the LORD, "You are my God;
> give ear, O LORD, to the voice of my supplications."
> O LORD, my Lord, my strong deliverer,
> you have covered my head in the day of battle.
> Do not grant, O LORD, the desires of the wicked;
> do not further their evil plot. (Psalm 140:6–8)

These covenant treaties between lord and vassal typically had six elements:

1. a preamble, which identified the suzerain or overlord by titles and ancestry;

2. a historical prologue, which described the past relationship between suzerain and vassal, emphasizing the suzerain's beneficence;

3. the stipulations assumed by both parties, but especially the obligations of the vassal toward the suzerain;

4. provision for the deposit—usually in the temple of the vassal's deity—and periodic reading of the treaty document;

5. a list of gods as witnesses, by whom both parties, but especially the vassal, swore allegiance to the treaty;

6. the list of curses and blessings accruing to the vassal for success or failure in complying with the treaty's stipulations.[2]

"Cutting a covenant" through formula words and ceremonial ordeals was meant to benefit both parties involved. Simply performing the covenant rituals, however, didn't unconditionally grant one the blessings and protection of the lord described; both sides of the agreement needed to be maintained. An additional consideration was the threat of curses that could be inflicted if the oath of the covenant wasn't upheld by the vassal. Ritually such a curse was enacted by "cutting" apart an animal and placing its pieces on the ground. The parties committed by the covenant then walked between the pieces, reminding them of what would happen if they broke their pledge. "Those who transgressed my covenant and did not keep the terms of the covenant that they made before me, I will make like the calf when they cut it in two and passed between its parts" (Jeremiah 34:18). Upon entering a covenant relationship, it would not be wise to ignore the agreements and promises made, nor to take its stipulations or laws lightly. And so, with a background knowledge of ancient covenant treaties, it's easy to understand more clearly the Hebrew concepts of God as lord, the kingdom of God, servants of the lord, having the law written on one's heart, being "cut off" from protection, and being "saved" by one's lord.

A Covenant with God

From the initial accounts of God's establishment of the human race, the Hebrew scriptures use the covenantal concept in defining their people's relationship with their God *YHWH*. (Although "Yahweh" is God's personal name, historically the word has at times been rendered, out of reverence, as "Adonai," or "Lord."[3]) The initial command at the creation to "fill the earth and master it" parallels the vassal's responsibility to his lord concerning the territory entrusted to him (Genesis 1:28, JPS). Adam and Eve turn away from their intimate face-to-face relationship with God and the guidelines for living in the garden—the heart of God's kingdom. But the covenant relationship is seen to continue and is especially evident during key events like these.

Noah and the flood

[God said to Noah,] "For my part, I am going to bring a flood of waters on the earth, to destroy from under heaven all flesh in which is the breath of life; everything that is on the earth shall die. But I will establish my covenant with you; and you shall come into the ark, you, your sons, your wife, and your sons' wives with you. . . . " Noah did this; he did all that God commanded him. . . . [Later] God said, "I establish my covenant with you, that never again shall all flesh be cut off by the waters of a flood, and never again shall there be a flood to destroy the earth." God said, "This is the sign of the covenant that I make between me and you and every living creature that is with you, for all future generations: I have set my bow in the clouds, and it shall be a sign of the covenant between me and the earth." (Genesis 6:17–18, 22; 9:11–13)

Abraham and circumcision

God said to Abraham, "As for you, you shall keep my covenant, you and your offspring after you throughout their generations. This is my covenant, which you shall keep, between me and you and your offspring after you: Every male among you shall be circumcised. You shall circumcise the flesh of your foreskins, and it shall be a sign of the covenant between me and you. . . . So shall my covenant be in your flesh an everlasting covenant." (Genesis 17:9–11, 13b)

Moses and the Law

Moses took half of the blood and put it in basins, and half of the blood he dashed against the altar. Then he took the book of the covenant, and read it in the hearing of the people; and they said, "All that the LORD has spoken we will do, and we will be obedient." Moses took the blood and dashed it on the people, and said, "See the blood of the covenant that the LORD has made with you in accordance with all these words." (Exodus 24:6–8)

David and kingship

The Lord said to Solomon, "As for you, if you will walk before me, as David your father walked, with integrity of heart and uprightness, doing according to all that I have commanded you, and keeping my statues and my ordinances, then I will establish your royal throne over Israel forever, as I promised your father David, saying, 'There shall not fail you a successor on the throne of Israel.' If you turn aside from following me, you or your children, and do not keep my commandments and my statutes that I have set before you, but go and serve other gods and worship them, then I will cut Israel off from the land I have given them . . ." (1 Kings 9:4–7a)

[God said,] "I have found David, son of Jesse, to be a man after my heart, who will carry out all my wishes." (Acts 13:22b)

A Future Covenant

The prophet Jeremiah even speaks of a future, more perfect, covenantal relationship:

But this is the covenant that I will make with the house of Israel after those days, says the LORD: I will put my law within them, and I will write it on their hearts; and I will be their God, and they shall be my people. (Jeremiah 31:33)

Influenced by the cultures in which they were immersed, the Hebrew people found the covenant analogy helpful in defining and describing their relationship with Yahweh. Into these accounts they further incorporated the unique and personal experiences with their God. Most notable is their way of relating to the most powerful lord. For them this alliance is not simply one of fear and the hope of protection; the bond is one initiated and lived out by Yahweh, himself, in terms of *hesed*. This Hebrew term incorporates the concepts of fidelity, judgment, and righteousness, as well as the will to save. Sometimes translated as *mercy or loving-kindness*, this attentiveness of God to his people can be referred to as "covenant love."[4] The choice to enter into such a covenant, the choice to live and love within God's kingdom, is one that's made freely. Verna Dozier writes:

> The heart of the relationship between God and human beings is freedom. Freedom is the image of God in the human creature. God freely chose to create. . . . I do not think these are esoteric assertions, the meat of irrelevant theological disputes. I think they are at the heart of the biblical understanding of God. A lonely God, a vulnerable God, a God who loves.[5]

Establishing a New Covenant

Relationships, people, and cultures aren't static, so the covenant was accepted, but also misunderstood, and then rejected many times throughout history. Jesus brought a new clarification of Yahweh's offer of a covenant alliance.

> Q. *What is the New Covenant?*
> A. *The New Covenant is the new relationship with God given by Jesus Christ, the Messiah, to the apostles; and, through them, to all who believe in him.*
> Q. *What did the Messiah promise in the New Covenant?*
> A. *Christ promised to bring us into the kingdom of God and give us life in all its fullness.*
> Q. *What response did Christ require?*
> A. *Christ commanded us to believe in him and to keep his commandments.*
> (BCP, 850–851)

Jesus' concept of the covenant wasn't all that new. The gospel examples, such as entrusting servants with talents (Matthew 25:14ff), initiating a covenant lawsuit by sending messengers to the tenants of the vineyard (Luke 20:9ff), and referring to himself as the son sent as judge (John 5:22–30) show Jesus' familiarity with the overlord system. And Jesus' listeners, too, would understand these narratives. They would know that "when a vassal failed to satisfy the obligations of the sworn treaty, the suzerain instituted a covenant lawsuit against him. The legal process was conducted by messengers. In the first of its two distinct phases messengers delivered one or more warnings. . . . If the messenger of the great king was rejected, imprisoned, and especially if he was killed, the legal process moved into its next phase. This was the declaration of war as an execution of the sacred sanctions of the treaty."[6]

The gospels also show that Jesus tried to alert the people of his time to the true meaning of the covenant: it wasn't just following laws or stipulations, or simply going through the ritual motions of the traditions.

> Now when the Pharisees and some of the scribes who had come from Jerusalem gathered around him [Jesus], they noticed that some of his

disciples were eating with defiled hands, that is, without washing them. (For the Pharisees, and all the Jews, do not eat unless they thoroughly wash their hands, thus observing the tradition of the elders; and they do not eat anything from the market unless they wash it; and there are also many other traditions that they observe, the washing of cups, pots, and bronze kettles.)

So the Pharisees and the scribes asked him, "Why do your disciples not live according to the tradition of the elders, but eat with defiled hands?" He said to them, "Isaiah prophesied rightly about you hypocrites, as it is written,

> 'This people honors me with their lips,
> but their hearts are far from me;
> in vain do they worship me,
> teaching human precepts as doctrines.'

You abandon the commandment of God and hold to human tradition." (Mark 7:1–8)

Jesus spoke of a loving, merciful, yet righteous God in a personal and relational way. Further, he invited his disciples to come and meet the Father through his own union with God.

[Jesus said,] "All things have been handed over to me by my Father; and no one knows who the Son is except the Father, or who the Father is except the Son and anyone to whom the Son chooses to reveal him." Then turning to the disciples, Jesus said to them privately, "Blessed are the eyes that see what you see! For I tell you that many prophets and kings desired to see what you see, but did not see it, and to hear what you hear, but did not hear it." (Luke 10:22–24)

Jesus' covenantal rules for living inside the kingdom were Yahweh's own directions of covenant love: "'You shall love the Lord your God with all your heart, and with all your soul, and with all your mind.' This is the greatest and first commandment. And a second is like it: 'You shall love your neighbor as yourself'" (Matthew 22:37–39; Deuteronomy 6:5; Leviticus 19:18). The concept wasn't new at all; the difference was, rather than simply obeying the man-made traditional laws, Jesus consciously and purposefully lived in true relationship with Yahweh (Mark 7:8; 1:22). This powerful relationship is witnessed by Jesus' prayers, teachings, and miracles—indeed throughout his whole life, death, and resurrection (John 8:29). By inviting others to enter the kingdom and accepting its covenant, the Jesus of the Gospels brought the reality of the relationship with Yahweh into the lives of the people he met. Accepting Jesus' invitation would be an alliance with Yahweh, truly a life-changing decision.

Key to Jesus' fulfilling his covenant was that he lived the relationship as the true and faithful servant of his lord. His work was Yahweh's, not simply his own (Mark 14:36). Likewise, Jesus often reminded his disciples to become *diakonoi* ("servants" or "ministers") themselves (Mark 10:35–45; Luke 9:46–48; Luke 22:24–27). Being a faithful servant of the lord, as well as a loyal citizen of the kingdom, are essential elements in a covenant relationship. And yet in Mark's Gospel, when Jesus spoke about the kingdom of God and what it was like, to him the lord of this covenantal kingdom was "Papa" (*Abba*—Mark 14:36). In fact, a stern father *can* be a lord; and a loving, yet challenging, king *can* be perceived as a dad (2 Samuel 7:14–15). And so in the language of the overlord and vassal covenant, the treaty partners referred to each other as "father" and "son" respectively.[7] Indeed, in that culture it wasn't unheard of for valuable and loyal slaves or servants to be adopted and become heirs.[8] Intriguingly, therefore, the concepts of servant and sonship, as well as friendship, aren't intrinsically opposed. This type of progression is evident in John's Gospel, which speaks of the relationship between Jesus and his disciples: "I do not call you servants[9] any longer, because the servant does not know what the master is doing; but I have called you friends, because I have made known to you everything that I have heard from my Father" (John 15:15. See also Romans 8:12–17; Galatians 3:26–4:7; James 2:5).

In addition to these examples of living the covenantal relationship, the synoptic gospels consistently portray Jesus as using the specific language of covenant: "Then he took a cup, and after giving thanks he gave it to them, and all of them drank from it. He said to them, 'This is my blood of the covenant, which is poured out for many. Truly I tell you, I will never again drink of the fruit of the vine until that day when I drink it new in the kingdom of God'" (Mark 14:23–25). The sacrificial slaughter that takes place to ratify the covenant alludes to the fate of the person who would break the covenant, but in sharing the resulting meal the parties are inseparably bound together as a new union. In the Hebrew practice:

> When God had received his share of the victim, the ones who had presented it ate the remainder in a sacrificial meal. The fact that the one victim had both been offered to God and eaten by the worshipers brought the two parties together in a spiritual communion, establishing and consolidating the covenant bond between the two. This was a joyful occasion . . .[10]

Perhaps it was Jesus' use of a *covenantal* ceremony that opened the eyes of those he broke bread with in the Emmaus resurrection account. The elements of the covenant ritual are those highlighted in this account: "When he was at the table with them, he took bread, *gave thanks, broke it* and began to *give it to them*. Then their eyes were opened and they recognized him, and he disappeared from their sight. . . . Then the two told what had happened on the way, and how Jesus was recognized by them when he broke the bread" (Luke 24:30–31, 35 NIV; emphasis added).

According to the account in Luke's Gospel, on the way to Emmaus Jesus had explained the scriptures that told how the Messiah had to suffer and then enter his glory (Luke 24:13–27). Such reflection and interpretation of the Hebrew Scriptures is evident, too, when Matthew's Gospel puts a self-accusation on the lips of the crowd that recalls the rituals of covenant in an ironic way. Moses "took the book of the covenant, and read it in the hearing of the people; and they said, 'All that the LORD has spoken we will do, and we will be obedient.' Moses took the blood and dashed it on the people, and said, 'See the blood of the covenant that the LORD has made with you in accordance with all these words'" (Exodus 24:7–8). Moses' dashing the blood on the people to ratify the covenant is paralleled by the people's response to Pilate regarding the responsibility of Jesus' death: "His blood be on us and on our children!" The people, even by attempting to break the covenant by "cutting themselves off" from Jesus and the truth of his message regarding God's covenant love, became participants in the very sacrifice that binds the new covenant (Matthew 27:22–25). Indeed, the early church understood and accepted Jesus' death as the sacrifice that sealed the new covenant: Christ "is the mediator of a new covenant, so that those who are called may receive the promised eternal inheritance, because a death has occurred that redeems them from the transgressions under the first covenant" (Hebrews 9:15).

A Covenant Community in the Early Church

As the disciples dealt with Jesus' death, the empty tomb, and the resurrection appearances, they realized the importance of spending time together in prayer and mutual support (John 20:19, 26; Acts 1:12–14). They became a "Christian" community, centered around their experience of Jesus as the promised Messiah—the Anointed One—the Christ. This community of believers was provided with the gift of the Holy Spirit for guidance: "I still have many things to say to you, but you cannot bear them now. When the Spirit of truth comes, he will guide you into all the truth . . ." (John 16:12–13a). Indeed, being thoroughly receptive to the Holy Spirit is necessary and natural to a genuine relationship with God in the spirit of Jesus' message of truth about Yahweh's covenant love.

The apostle Paul further describes the role of the Holy Spirit. For Paul the Spirit provides assistance and guidance for developing the proper interdependence of the people within the emerging early church assemblies: "Now there are varieties of gifts, but the same Spirit; and there are varieties of services, but the same Lord; and there are varieties of activities, but it is the same God who activates all of them in everyone. To each is given the manifestation of the Spirit for the common good" (1 Corinthians 12:4–7). "Since all have some function or responsibility to perform, there are no mere spectators in church but only active participants."[11] With each of its members empowered by the Spirit of God through the ritual of baptism, the early church recognized itself as the community of saints on earth. It was a holy gathering of Christians dedicated to Christ, and therefore a new earthly covenantal "Kingdom of God."[12]

The statements of the early church fathers reflect the richness of meaning embraced in the developing Christian ritual sacrament of baptism. The early rites were developed to allow the neophytes or new Christians to experience what couldn't be explained. As the church movement grew, some ceremonies that developed were specific to particular areas or cultures, but each practice was an attempt to convey through sacred action an inexpressible encounter with God. Imagine an adult convert to the emerging Christian faith being initiated through even just a few of these rituals described in the following writings from the first centuries of the Christian era:

- And the king gave orders that the bath should be closed for seven days, and that no man should bathe in it: and when the seven days were done, on the eighth day they three entered into the bath by night that Judas [Thomas] might baptize them. And many lamps were lighted in the bath.[13]
- As soon, then, as you entered, you put off your tunic. . . . Having stripped yourselves, you were naked. . . . O wondrous thing! You were naked in the sight of all, and were not ashamed. . . .[14]
- As if he were about to lead you into heaven itself by means of these rites, he prepares to anoint your whole body with this spiritual oil so that his unction may armor all your limbs and make them invulnerable to any weapons the Enemy may hurl.[15]
- Have you seen the terms of the contract? After the renunciation of the Evil One and all the works he delights in, the priest instructs you to speak again as follows: *And I pledge myself, Christ, to you.*[16]
- And each of you was asked, whether he believed in the name of the Father, and of the Son, and of the Holy Spirit, and you made that saving confession, and descended three times into the water and ascended again. . . .[17]
- After this white robes were given to you as a sign that you were putting off the covering of sins, and putting on the chaste veil of innocence . . .[18]
- Then, when we are taken up (as new-born children), we taste first of all a mixture of milk and honey . . .[19]
- And you were first anointed on the forehead, that you might be delivered from the shame. . . . Then on your ears; that you might receive the ears which are quick to hear the Divine Mysteries. . . . Then on the nostrils; that receiving the sacred ointment you may say, *We are to God a sweet savor of Christ, in them that are saved.* Afterwards on your breast; that having put on the *breast-plate of righteousness, you may stand against the wiles of the devil.* . . . Having been counted worthy of this Holy Chrism, you are called Christians, verifying the name also by your new birth.[20]
- Then the Deacon cries aloud, "Receive you one another; and let us

kiss one another." Think not that this kiss is of the same character with those given in public by common friends. It is not such: but this kiss blends souls one with another, and courts entire forgiveness for them. The kiss therefore is the sign that our souls are mingled together, and banish all remembrance of wrongs. . . . The kiss therefore is reconciliation, and for this reason holy. . . .[21]

Thus there did develop a proliferation of practices that also included such traditions as: preparatory fasting, multiple anointings, the use of sack cloth in the ceremony, and even foot washing. In addition, lengthy theological discussions ensued about details such as: which days were appropriate for baptisms, when exactly the Holy Spirit was imparted, each of the specific resulting effects of the sacrament, and the ongoing transformation of the newly baptized. It was understood, however, that the essential elements of all these beliefs and ceremonies could be found in the use of water and the Trinitarian formula:

But you shall beforehand anoint the person with holy oil, and afterward baptize him with water, and in the conclusion shall seal him with the ointment, that the anointing with oil may be the participation of the Holy Spirit, and the water the symbol of the death, and the ointment the seal of the covenants. But if there be neither oil nor ointment, water is sufficient both for the anointing, and for the seal, and for the confession of Him that is dead, or indeed is dying together with Christ.[22]

The Baptismal Covenant

The focus was to be not on the rites themselves, but the candidate's developing relationship with God. "In baptism, the candidate submits to the water, which is both threatening and life-giving. . . . Baptism brings us face to face with the uncertainty and dependency of our lives and helps us to understand that this place of apparent danger and death is really an encounter with the LOVE that sustains us in life."[23] Baptism with water as well as the Holy Spirit and fire, as an ordeal, as a consecration, and as a cleansing was recognized as the official means of entering the covenantal relationship with God and of being initiated into the growing and supportive Christian community.

> Q. *What is Holy Baptism?*
> A. *Holy Baptism is the sacrament by which God adopts us as his children and makes us members of Christ's Body, the Church, and inheritors of the kingdom of God.*
> Q. *What is the outward and visible sign in Baptism?*
> A. *The outward and visible sign in Baptism is water, in which the person is baptized in the Name of the Father, and of the Son, and of the Holy Spirit.*

17

Q. *What is the inward and spiritual grace in Baptism?*

    A. *The inward and spiritual grace in Baptism is union with Christ in his death and resurrection, birth into God's family the Church, forgiveness of sins, and new life in the Holy Spirit.*

Q. *What is required of us at Baptism?*

    A. *It is required that we renounce Satan, repent of our sins, and accept Jesus as our Lord and Savior.*

        (BCP, 858)

A savior is the one who comes when you're surrounded by the enemy, showing you the way to safety and strength. This person is your "Lord." The early Christians experienced Jesus as the one who saves, as the lord who administered the benefits and protection of the covenant. He saved them from their enemy by rescuing them from the immanent evil forces they perceived and by uniting them with God through the incarnation. The Gospel of Luke summarizes this understanding in a prophecy regarding Jesus spoken by John the Baptist's father Zechariah:

> *"Blessed be the Lord God of Israel,*
> *for he has looked favorably on his people and redeemed them.*
> *He has raised up a mighty savior for us*
> *in the house of his servant David,*
> *as he spoke through the mouth of his holy prophets from of old,*
> *that we would be saved from our enemies*
> *and from the hand of all who hate us.*
> *Thus he has shown the mercy promised to our ancestors,*
> *and has remembered his holy covenant,*
> *the oath that he swore to our ancestor Abraham,*
> *to grant us that we, being rescued from the hands of our enemies,*
> *might serve him without fear, in holiness and righteousness*
> *before him all our days. . . ."* (Luke 1:68–75)

Initially this realization of Jesus as savior was experienced in a direct relationship with him or close to it, through the testimony of the apostles, or by the witness of the disciples or other charter-member Christians. Through consciously choosing baptism, the early converts professed their belief in Jesus as Lord and Savior, were dedicated to God, rejected their evil habits,[24] received the gift of the Holy Spirit, and became consecrated as members of the sacred assembly, the kingdom of God. Thus baptism was established and understood by the early Christians as a covenant—a relationship initiated by God, to which there is a response in faith.[25] Further, this initiation, as a covenant-making ceremony, was not complete without a formal thanksgiving (*eucharistia* or "Eucharist") for the Lord God's past benevolent deeds and a communal sacrificial meal binding all of the community's members together with their Lord in covenantal union.[26]

The Organized Community

Being bound together in Christ is the natural state of a Christian community. A person is introduced to Jesus by his followers—other Christians. And it is with the aid of the Holy Spirit and the support of the resulting group of like-minded people that the new Christian is able to reorganize his or her life in terms of God's values. The new convert wishes to accept God's offer of a covenant union and thus enter into God's kingdom. When these early Christians gathered it was referred to by the common name for an assembly of people—*ekklesia* or the "ecclesiastical" church.

> Q. **What is the Church?**
> A. *The Church is the community of the New Covenant. . . . .*
> Q. **What is the mission of the Church?**
> A. *The mission of the Church is to restore all people to unity with God and each other in Christ.*
> Q. **Through whom does the Church carry out its mission?**
> A. *The Church carries out its mission through the ministry of all its members.*
>   (BCP, 854–855)

The excitement of Jesus' message, the reality of God's presence and love, and the empowerment of the Holy Spirit are evident in the writings of the early church. Eventually, though, the experience of immanence wore off and the Christian communities shifted their focus to the performance of traditions, maintenance of the institution, and the defense of specific beliefs. Thus the church as a structured, organizational entity emerged with inclinations and concerns of its own. This shift can be seen in many aspects of the church's emerging practices in the early centuries, such as in the employment of a few approved and specially trained professional priests, reserving study of the Bible for the clergy so that it would not be misinterpreted by those untrained, and use of an academic language with a theology based on logic and deduction. This organizational emphasis resulted in the people's loss of direct listening and learning from the apostles' teaching and scriptures, the laying aside of the vernacular, parables, and real-life experiences, as well as an abandonment of a personal encounter with God that had been earlier evidenced by gifts from the Holy Spirit.

Questions for Reflection

1. Have you seen your Christian commitment as an active "covenant with God"? Why or why not?

2. How does understanding the ancient practices of covenant and baptism assist you in determining your future path?

19

CHAPTER 3

The Church: Spirit-led People in an Organized Structure

The Church reformed, but always reforming

(Reformation motto, circa 1500–1650 CE)

Although the reason for the Christian community's existence is to focus on God—"restoring all people to unity with God and each other in Christ" (BCP, 855)—the church, as a human institution, also looks to itself as it organizes its members and structures their activities.

Almost every sociologist believes that as people interact, social patterns will develop among them and become an important influence over their actions. Indeed, these patterns distinguish a "bunch of individuals" from some form of organization such as a society. A social pattern means that social interaction is made regular, it is regulated, and a stability is established whereby individual actors know what they are to do in relation to one another. Social patterns are routines, common expectations, predictable behaviors, and ways of thinking and acting that have been established so that ongoing cooperation is made possible. People get used to the ideas, rules, and actions that they use over and over, and people depend on their continuation so that interaction runs smoothly. The longer the interaction and the more isolated it is, the more likely the patterns will take hold. As new people enter the interaction they learn the patterns. Patterns are anchored in the past. They are taken for granted.[1]

The church as a group of interacting people has developed such social patterns. At times, though, these patterns can be somewhat complex and then the expectations are not as clear-cut as might be presumed. One example of this is the tendency for the church to shift focus between an emphasis on developing the relationship with God and an inclination to prioritize organizing relationships among the church members themselves. This fluctuation can be seen as a natural polarity within the make-up of the church. According to Barry Johnson, a polarity is defined as an issue that is both ongoing and has interdependent poles.[2] A polarity is not a problem to be solved; instead, it is a symbiotic relationship calling for ongoing shifting and balancing. "A key principle of polarity theory states: Problems can be solved; conflicts can be resolved; but polarities can only be managed. Polarities are unsolvable and unavoidable. Your only choice is whether you will manage them well or manage them poorly."[3] The following diagram, provided by Roy Oswald of the Alban Institute, illustrates the "Focus of Ministry" within the church as a polarity, with "Movement" and "Enterprise" as the defining poles.[4]

Figure 1. Focus of Ministry Polarity

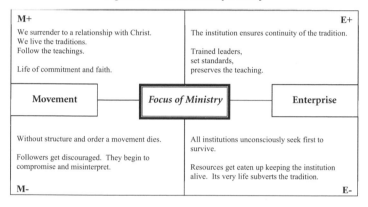

Notice that each pole has both positive and negative characteristics. This particular dynamic starts on the Movement side of the polarity. Movements are often thought of as social events characterized by positive energy, high commitment, and a personal attachment to the founder or leader. Once the initial experience subsides, however, often the group encounters negative elements such as being sidetracked, discouraged, or dispirited. In response to this turn of events, some dedicated members may take positive action, gathering together the individual elements of the movement into histories, traditions, and statements of belief, thus preserving the experience. But, in this very process the entity is no longer a movement but has become much like a business enterprise; it is an institution concerned now with survival. Survival itself is not negative, but the danger is that the primary focus can easily switch from the original ideals and loyalty to the founder, to simply a self-focused institution concerned with ongoing maintenance and dealing with issues of legalism and stagnation. Both of the elements of this pole, Movement and Enterprise, are defining elements of the church's ministry. Therefore, both poles need to be acknowledged and then managed well by applying the counter balance when appropriate. Throughout the rest of this work, I will use [**M**] to

21

refer to Movement/God-focused elements and [E] to indicate the Enterprise/Business/Organization elements of the church. A plus (+) or minus (-) will refer to either their positive or negative quadrant.

The balancing process works like this:
- A congregation in the movement/positive quadrant [M+] "refers often to the Scriptures and feels a direct link with the founder."
- In the movement/negative quadrant [M-], there is discouragement and misinterpretation as the intimate relationship is lost.
- If a community then moves to the institution/positive quadrant [E+], the "continuity of the faith is ensured" by the preservation of the Scriptures and professional training for the leaders.
- Ultimately, though, there is movement to the negative aspect of the institution/negative quadrant [E-]: "Faith becomes weak, and the institution becomes self-serving."
- From here the best move is back to the positive aspects of the movement side of the polarity [M+] and a reconnection with the founder.
- And so on . . .; continuing to move to the opposite pole when necessary in order to counteract negative elements and maintain a balance.[5]

Thus to manage such a polarity well, the Christian church community needs to stay primarily in the two positive quadrants. This promotes a strengthening rather than a deterioration of the relational organization.[6] By acknowledging this polarity in the church, it is possible for creative solutions to form by merging the sacred focus with its positive, though secular, institutional elements. For example, when members' concentration on a topic becomes too narrow and God's teachings become misinterpreted—Movement's negative pole [M-]—an appropriate response would be "Point of order: We need to pray." This effectively moves the group to the upper opposite pole—Enterprise's orderliness [E+]—and balances it with a call to refocus through prayer on relationship with God and on God's intentions [M+].

The back and forth struggle between an imperfect people seeking an intimate relationship with God, and human society attempting to ensure survival for itself through order, structure, and organization, can be seen repeatedly throughout salvation history. There are many scriptural examples. Moses gathered seventy elders to share in both the Spirit of God [M+] and in the burden of guiding the people [E+] (Numbers 11:16–17). The Hebrews desired a human king (who would enslave them and take their belongings) [E-] rather than the divine king [M+] (1 Samuel 8:1–22). Josiah's reforms upon finding the book of the covenant illustrate an adjustment from the M- quadrant of false gods to an attempt to balance the E+ and M+ quadrants (2 Kings 22–23). Yahweh's advice given through the prophet Jeremiah to those in exile [E-] contains the language of this polarity as well: "Build houses and live in them; plant gardens and eat what they produce. Take wives and have sons and daughters . . . . seek the welfare of the city . . . for in its welfare you will find your welfare [E+]. . . . Then when you call upon me and come and pray to me, I will hear you. When you search for me, you will find me; if you seek me with all your heart [M+]" (Jeremiah 29:5–7, 12–13).

The Gospels show that Jesus, too, dealt with this polarity by maintaining a sense of focus as well as organization within his group of followers. He strongly objected to the legalistic, man-made traditions that the Pharisees thought important for keeping things orderly [E-] (Matthew 15:1–20). Disregarding the Pharisees' inordinate laws, however, did not give rise to chaos. Jesus "disrupted the religious systems precisely in order to reemphasize the fundamental priesthood to draw attention away from the religious model and back to the true encounter with the HOLY in the context of ordinary human existence" [from E- to M+].[7] So, too, Jesus' followers were an organized group. According to the Gospel accounts, he trained and sent them on assignments or missions (Matthew 10:1); the disciples were assigned to crowd control and litter duty (Mark 6:39–44); they made travel arrangements (Matthew 21:1ff) and meal preparations (Matthew 26:17ff); one was in charge of the finances (John 12:6; 13:29); and various donors provided for further needs as well (Matthew 27:55–56; Luke 8:1–3) [E+]. Jesus, however, proclaimed his organizational structure to be based, not on the human desire for control or power, but rather on service to God (Mark 10:42–45) [M+]. "The practices of governance Jesus commended did not match the prevailing versions and evidently were not supposed to. Rather than shaping his followers into the usual hierarchy of power, Jesus constituted his community around power turned upsidedown."[8]

The early church also experienced both sides of this polarity. "These are the ideas left to us by the early churches: the importance of church structure; the church as a community, corporate but not institutional; the movement of the Spirit; the people of God; the necessity for a personal relationship to Jesus; and a high respect for law and authority."[9] In time, however, the church inevitably shifted more toward the institutional pole, and the resulting unbalance did not go unnoticed. Often groups, such as the monastics as well as other charismatic leaders, attempted to refocus the community back on the basic Christian values.[10] But these movements resulted in organizations that tended over time to shift to the institutional pole as well. The Reformation, its modifications, and the resulting denominational organizations also can be seen to follow this pattern. In fact, *ecclsia reformata, sed semper reformanda* (the church reformed, but always reforming), the rallying cry of the Reformation, speaks of the need to constantly manage the polarity of the church's focus. And in the Reformation the image of God's covenant with the people was again brought to the fore: "The concept of a 'relationship of mutual responsibility,' contingent not only on the faithfulness of God but also upon that of man provided the Reformation with a most useful means of articulating its history and identity."[11]

For Anglicans "theological and ethical issues are resolved through decisions concerning liturgy more than doctrine."[12] And it is through the revised rituals and a new emphasis on catechesis that the beliefs of the Reformers and the resulting sacramental reforms [all E+] were conveyed to the people in the pew. But despite all the effort on the part of the theologians of the time to reform the baptismal rites, little actually changed in the lives of the people.[13] This is not surprising, however, for according to Barry Johnson's view: "In a well-managed polarity most time is spent experiencing the positive aspects of one pole or the other. When the downside of a pole is experienced, it is used as a signal to move to the positive of the other pole."[14] The goal, therefore, would be, not just to revitalize or reform the ritual or institutional elements of the church, but to balance both spiritual renewal and structural reorganization. This needs to be done in a way that would allow these two poles to flow back and forth and in the process enhance each other. It is upon the recognition of a relationship of mutual responsiveness and responsibility that ongoing reformation is to be based. Therefore, efforts to improve the structure or success of the institution (including the efficacy of its ritual formulas) [E+] will not have lasting effects unless there is also an ongoing openness to the Holy Spirit and a refocusing and recommitment to a covenantal partnership with God, as well as an acceptance of the responsibility on the part of each member that such a commitment entails [M+]. Verna Dozier expresses this polarity when she writes: "I believe that the church, in whatever form it appears institutionally, rejects the dream of God. The paradox is that within that institution the dream is kept."[15]

As a refocusing on God, rather than on institution, progresses, it becomes apparent that the image of God is reflected in *all* persons. Theologians agree that this image is established through creation, fully realized in the incarnation, and confirmed through the empowerment of the Holy Spirit. In avowing God's presence in each person, each is recognized to have inherent worth (worthiness) and dignity, as well as acknowledged to possess consequential responsibility and accountability. The Episcopal Church can be seen to be moving more specifically in this direction from the 1950s on, as the canons start to reflect the practice of *non-ordained* church members (and particularly women) taking on significant active roles of leadership and participation in the liturgy. Contributing throughout the liturgy by reading the epistle, presenting offerings of their earnings as well as the bread and wine, and administering the chalice, all "reflect a growing understanding that the eucharist is . . . an action involving the whole congregation."[16] This atmosphere was the backdrop against which the 1979 Book of Common Prayer was being developed.

> Through the long process leading to the 1979 revision of The Book of Common Prayer, the rites of initiation were given special attention. As a result, The Book of Common Prayer establishes the centrality and foundational character of Holy Baptism, describing it as the sacrament by which God adopts us as God's children, binds us into community, and makes us members of Christ's body. Through baptism we are made members of one another, and corporately we become Christ's body or

presence in the world. Baptism is our common ordination to ministry and, therefore, is the keystone to personal and congregational renewal.

In baptism God binds the divine self to us with a covenant promise, and our life in Christ begins. Over and over again in ever maturing ways, we respond by confessing our faith and promising obedience. God's promises are forever, so baptism is never to be repeated. But our human promises are not once and for all, so baptismal renewal is never ending.[17]

Initiated through use of the 1979 Book of Common Prayer, the language of "baptismal covenant," "baptismal identity," "baptismal commitment," and "baptismal ministry" has been emphasized in the Episcopal Church for the past twenty-five years. By placing baptism at the forefront of the church's life, a movement has been started to advance beyond a church of separate lay and ordained categories toward truly becoming individuals covenanted with God and the Christian community through baptism. Through the baptismal covenant each baptized person formally responds to Jesus' invitation and enters life in God's kingdom. Each promises to share in the loving service of the Lord, God. Each accepts joint responsibility for mission and ministry by embracing the gift of the Holy Spirit. This ministry is to be undertaken, not just in and through the limited world of the church institution, but throughout God's realm—to the ends of the earth.

Questions for Reflection

1. Do your own talents lie more on the Movement side (meditation and prayer, introducing people to Jesus, calling people back to God, following the Spirit) or Enterprise side (setting up programs of study, organizing worship services, following the traditions) of the Focus of Ministry polarity?

Name at least one person you know who works best on the other side of the polarity as yourself.

2. In which of the four quadrants do you see your congregation currently functioning? According to the polarity theory, which quadrant(s) should it move to in order to move in a healthy direction?

List a few specific concrete steps your church could take to move into a healthier balance. (Examples include: Bible study, vocational discernment, reconciliation service, faith sharing, prayer teams, exercises to deepen basic faith, programs for adult faith formation, retreats, parish renewal programs, and so on.)

SECTION TWO

THE EPISCOPAL CHURCH AND THE BAPTISMAL COVENANT

A Sermon on the Baptism of Jesus and Renewal of Baptismal Covenant

Let us join with those who are committing themselves to Christ and renew our own baptismal covenant.

(BCP, 303)

The 1979 Book of Common Prayer invites the whole congregation to renew its baptismal covenant in the context of the Eucharist each time a baptism is held. The prayer book also promotes several occasions throughout the year as fitting for recommitment by the local Christian community, even if no one is being presented for the actual sacrament at the time (BCP, 312). The following is a sample of the type of sermon that can be used on such an occasion.

Beginning Prayer

"Almighty and eternal God, so draw our hearts to you, so guide our minds, so fill our imaginations, so control our wills, that we may be wholly yours, utterly dedicated to you; and then use us, we pray you, as you will, and always to your glory and the welfare of all your people; through our Lord and Savior Jesus Christ. Amen." (BCP, 832–833, #61)

Please be seated.

Body of Sermon

Now, today's Gospel reading is about Jesus' relationship with John the Baptist. Why did Jesus go to John to be baptized? Why do we get baptized and have our children baptized? What does baptism mean in the Episcopal tradition? Does it mean anything at all? My boss, who is the son of a Baptist minister, told me that when he and his wife attended the Episcopal baptism of his nephew here in town, he was quite surprised to hear the priest say, "Baptism doesn't mean anything—it's just something we do." Luckily, the archdeacon was there and spoke up and addressed the true meaning of baptism. How about you—what would you say if someone asked you, "What does baptism mean?" What would you say? (Ask the congregation for input and repeat the answers so all can hear. Possible responses may include the following concepts:)

- It's for the forgiveness of sin.
- Some use it as a name-giving ceremony.
- Some people ask me to do it for them so their children will be saved (as an insurance policy).
- We do it to become members of the community, the church.
- It's a way to be dedicated to God.
- My mom told me that it was to take away original sin.
- It makes us children of God.
- Baptism lets us be a witness to the world.
- In it we receive the Holy Spirit.

Good! All of these are part of the whole meaning. If you look in the Book of Common Prayer's Catechism on page 858, it says: "Holy Baptism is the sacrament by which God adopts us as his children and makes us members of Christ's Body, the Church, and inheritors of the kingdom of God."

The baptism that Jesus received from John was similar. But John's baptism was referred to as the "Baptism of Repentance"—typical of Jewish baptism rituals— and it involved the forgiveness of sin; it was a rite of purification. And that can be confusing because some of us wonder, "What did Jesus have to be 'repentant' about?" And sometimes that's our focus, too—repentance—because we worry so much about missing the mark and not being perfect. But remember, forgiveness is reconciliation. It restores one's relationship with another and that's the big picture: one's relationship with God, turning back to God, and God's forgiveness and mercy. "God adopts us, makes us members of Christ's Body, and inheritors of God's Kingdom!" (BCP, 858). In the Episcopal tradition we talk about the "Baptismal Covenant." This concept of covenant helps define our relationship with God.

The type of covenant that we're talking about isn't an agreement between two equal partners like in a business agreement or in the marriage ritual. It's based on the Hebrew covenant with Yahweh, which was similar to the typical ancient Near Eastern treaty used between a lord and his vassals or tenants. There was a solemn, ritualized formula for affirming these covenants:

- First the preamble would identify the Great King—the one who initiated the treaty.

- Then the prologue would list all the benefits given to the vassal in the past by this lord.
- Next, the stipulations were spelled out. These were rules like, "Don't make any treaties with other kingdoms."
- There was a public proclamation of the oath with a list of witnesses.
- There were lists of curses and blessings. The ritual sacrifice illustrates this concept of curse: "as this animal was slaughtered so shall be he who breaks this covenant." (Lord, have mercy!)
- Then, finally, the sacrificed animal became a ritual meal. By eating together, those who shared the life that had just ended formed a new life, a new community together, bound as one by the new covenant.

Remember the Ten Commandments? Listen to how they were ratified or adopted:

Moses took half of the blood [of the sacrificed bull] and put it in basins, and half of the blood he dashed against the altar. Then he took the book of the covenant, and read it in the hearing of the people; and they said, "All that the LORD has spoken we will do, and we will be obedient." Moses took the blood and dashed it on the people, and said, "See the blood of the covenant that the LORD has made with you in accordance with all these words." (Exodus 24:6–8)

So as long as the vassal or the servant remained faithful to the lord and the promises, he and his family could expect a good relationship with his lord—one of friendship, peace, and protection. If, however, the vassal broke off on his own or switched over to a different lord, he would have been confronted with the vengeance as spelled out in the oath of the covenant. This wasn't just a 10 percent financial obligation: this was a 100 percent "stand-with-you-in-battle" commitment. This was an issue of *loyalty*—devoted vassals committed themselves to ongoing, loving service to their lord.

It's important to understand the language of lords and kingdoms to understand what was going on in biblical times—to understand what the biblical writers and the Spirit are trying to tell us. This may seem like ancient history that doesn't apply to us anymore, but this language has to do with ancient truths, ageless alliances, the battle of good and evil. That's why movies like *The Lord of the Rings* are so popular: people are searching for ancient truths and sometimes it's too hard for us to see those truths when we're still involved in the battle itself.

Even in the New Testament this language is present: We speak of the Kingdom or Reign of God, and Christians are sometimes described as soldiers in the service of God in the battle between good and evil. In fact, the word *pagan* used to mean a regular citizen of a country, that is, a civilian. Eventually, the Christianized meaning became "those people who are not Christian soldiers"—those not part of God's Kingdom. The word *sacrament* from the Latin originally meant an oath of allegiance—a military oath. Much as the Hebrew concept of "covenant" was an oath to the great king, one's lord, a sacrament was an oath of loyalty and service to one's kingdom.

Gospel, you know, means "good news," right? But this term was specifically good news that was heralded or proclaimed, such as victory in battle. The battle of the God of mercy and love is, of course, against evil, against things like emptiness, apathy, superficiality, secrecy, nothingness, selfishness, and greed. We need not be captives of this evil. God, through Jesus, has won this battle; it is up to us to claim the victory and then enter the Kingdom!

So what then did Jesus' baptism mean? It was a public, ritual affirmation of Jesus' relationship with God. And so to ratify his covenant with his Father, Jesus presented himself publicly for John's ritual baptism—with John the Baptist and his disciples as witnesses—to make it known that Jesus was ready to do God's will to bring about the Kingdom. It wasn't so much about forgiveness of sin as it was about confirming his relationship with God. And what was God's response? "This is my son, the beloved, with whom I am well pleased!"

And, so, what does the Episcopal Baptismal Covenant mean for us here today? God reaches out and calls to each of us, offering loving protection and mercy, and then *we* are invited to respond. Then, if we believe, and if we respond affirmatively to God's invitation, we become partners in God's love, God's life, God's Kingdom, and God's service. And because it is a covenant, this is about a sacrifice, the end of a life, which seals such an important agreement. Only then does this sacrifice become a festive meal that celebrates the new life of those united through the covenant. Through death to life! Who dies? Jesus died. And each time we renew our relationship with God, *we* die; baptism with water and the Holy Spirit is a dangerous thing! Our old selfish selves die in order for our new selves to live more freely with our loving God.

For most of us our baptism happened long ago, but throughout the year, we in the Episcopal Church have the opportunity to renew and celebrate our baptismal commitment. Today, the celebration of the baptism of Jesus is one of those special days. So, in order to prepare, I invite you to join with me in a guided meditation.

Meditation

Start by closing your eyes.
Now think about yourself, about who you are,
your responsibilities and relationships:
- at home and with family members, with friends and animals.
- at school or work with clients, supervisors, and coworkers.
- in your neighborhood and in doing errands.
- in church and volunteering.

What are you concerned or worried about in your life?

What is important to you?

What makes you smile?

Now picture yourself hurrying at night to an important meeting. It's dark, but there's a light to guide you. Other people are gathering, too. You recognize some of the people—others are unfamiliar. You realize that this meeting is at a holy place, and you find that you are gathering around an altar of sacrifice, and you realize that God is there.

God notices you, too, and says, "I'm glad you came. Are you ready, then? There's much work to be done."

How do you feel?

What is your response to God?

What is the first thing that you know you must do?

And as you think about what this thing is, you realize that God will be there to help you through it.

Finally, think again about who you are:

you are God's beloved child,

you have been made in God's image,

you are beautiful.

Now, slowly open your eyes.

Renewal of Baptismal Covenant

We, too, have an altar to remind us of God's presence. And we know that God will help us in all that we have to do, here, standing in front of the altar, and out in the world standing in the midst of all God's people and in God's creation. In just a few minutes we'll stand, or kneel, before this altar and our priest's Eucharistic prayer will recount the blessings and benefits of our ancient covenant with God.

And then our ritual re-enactment of Jesus' last covenantal meal with his disciples will further bind us to God and each other.

And finally, you will be sent out on a mission in the world—back to your own specific area of service for God's Kingdom.

But right now it is time for each of you to publicly and ritualistically affirm your relationship with God through the renewal of your baptismal covenant. (Your responses can be found in the bulletin insert or in the Book of Common Prayer on page 292.)

Please stand and face the altar. [Priest here moves to the bowl of water and tree branch—first sprinkles the altar and then moves through the congregation sprinkling as the people renew their vows.]

Do you reaffirm your renunciation of evil and renew your commitment to Jesus Christ?

I do.

Do you believe in God the Father?

I believe in God, the Father almighty,
creator of heaven and earth.

Do you believe in Jesus Christ, the Son of God?

I believe in Jesus Christ, his only Son, our Lord.
He was conceived by the power of the Holy Spirit
and born of the Virgin Mary
He suffered under Pontius Pilate,
was crucified, died, and was buried.
He descended to the dead.
On the third day he rose again.
He ascended into heaven,
and is seated at the right hand of the Father.
He will come again to judge the living and the dead.

Do you believe in God the Holy Spirit?

I believe in the Holy Spirit,
the holy catholic Church,
the communion of saints,
the forgiveness of sins,
the resurrection of the body,
and the life everlasting.

Will you continue in the apostles' teaching and fellowship,
in the breaking of bread,
and in the prayers?

I will, with God's help.

Will you persevere in resisting evil, and,
whenever you fall into sin, repent and return to the Lord?

I will, with God's help.

Will you proclaim by word and example
the Good News of God in Christ?

I will, with God's help.

Will you seek and serve Christ
in all persons,
loving your neighbor as yourself?

I will, with God's help.

Will you strive for justice and peace among all people,
and respect the dignity of every human being?

I will, with God's help.

> [after congregation has been sprinkled, priest leaves the bowl of water in
> the baptismal font]

May Almighty God, the Father of our Lord Jesus Christ,
who has given us a new birth by water and the Holy Spirit,
and bestowed upon us the forgiveness of sins,
keep us in eternal life by his grace,
in Christ Jesus our Lord. *Amen.* (BCP 292–294)

The Peace

Now turn and look at all the people around you. These are just some of the people who stand before the altar of God to hear God's promise and to make a commitment to loving service. These people here are special to us, because today we stand before God's altar together. In the past, at each new baptism we have stood together and vowed to support these persons in their Christian life. Now, continue your support, as you greet each other in peace. **May the peace of the Lord be always with you.** *And also with you.*

(The above service was celebrated by the people of St. Stephen's Episcopal Church, in Phoenix, Arizona.[1] The rite for "The Renewal of Baptismal Vows" can be found in the Episcopal Book of Common Prayer on pages 292–294. The renewal of the baptismal covenant is most appropriate during the following services: Easter Vigil, Pentecost, All Saints' Day celebration, and the feast of the Baptism of our Lord.)

CHAPTER 4

The Study and Its Demographics

Yet because there is no remedy, but that of necessity there must be some rules; therefore certain rules are here set forth, which, as they be few in number; so they be plain and easy to be understood. So that here you have an order for prayer (as touching the reading of the holy Scripture), much agreeable to the mind and purpose of the old fathers, and a great deal more profitable and commodious, than that which of late was used. It is more profitable, because here are left out many things, whereof some be untrue, some uncertain, some vain and superstitious: and is ordained nothing to be read, but the very pure word of God, the holy Scriptures, or that which is evidently grounded upon the same; and that in such a language and order as is most easy and plain for the understanding, both of the readers and hearers. It is also more commodious, both for the shortness thereof, and for the plainness of the order, and for that the rules be few and easy. Furthermore, by this order the curates shall need none other books for their public service, but this book and the Bible: by the means whereof, the people shall not be at so great charge for books, as in time past they have been.

Book of Common Prayer, Preface, 1549

In 1979 the Episcopal Church produced a prayer book that put baptismal identity and ministry at the forefront of the church's life. By implication, this shift meant the Episcopal Church would become less a hierarchical structure and more a community of all the baptized sharing the responsibility for mission and ministry in God's service. After twenty-five years of this official stance, how much has it taken hold? This book is based on a thesis that examined how today's Episcopalians are living out their baptismal covenants following this new focus of baptismal renewal in the church. In light of this emphasis on the image of a baptismal covenant made with God, would the Episcopal congregations be ones where each and every member continuously made conscious decisions to follow Jesus' teachings and live as Christians each day? Would the covenantal promises be reflected in the choices made throughout each week as the members used their Spirit-given gifts throughout God's creation? Would the specific promises delineated and affirmed, since 1979, by the Episcopal baptismal rite be either used as a guideline, or obviously reflected in the people's daily actions? Also, in accepting and emphasizing the specific language and image of "covenant," the Episcopal Church in effect agreed to recognize God in terms of an immanent relationship and partnership. Would these covenantal promises, therefore, be conveyed with a humble attitude of standing alongside God, fulfilling the vows with God's help and in God's service to all of God's creation?

To assist in this analysis, during May 2002, I wrote to the one hundred domestic Episcopal dioceses of the United States, asking for recommendations of congregations where there has been significant lay development and involvement. One-third (thirty-four) of the diocesan offices supplied usable responses, with a total of fifty-eight congregations being recommended. The intent was to study the congregations themselves, but the responses from the diocesan offices were also interesting. Two separate responses from opposite ends of the country will illustrate one set of the extremes: (1) "Unfortunately we . . . do not have any parishes with significant lay involvement out in the community as a whole. We are working towards this and pray it will begin to happen in four to five years." (2) "We are happy to provide you with a list of the names, addresses and phone numbers for the congregations in this diocese." Neither of these responses provided usable data, since the first response informs me that this diocese has *no one* to recommend, while the second sent me a list of *all* of their congregations.

The fifty-eight congregations that were recommended then were directly asked for assistance with a study that was attempting to research lay involvement. (For the most part I refrained from using direct reference to "baptismal ministry," fearing that using those words might lead the respondent to give what they might perceive to be the "right" answer. Instead I chose to ask questions utilizing the more objective, but obviously rather vague, term "lay involvement.") Three things were requested: (1) complete a questionnaire, (2) send samples of written documents such as worship aids, newcomer's packets, mission statements, annual reports, and recent newsletters, and (3) provide a knowledgeable person who would be willing to be interviewed. Topics covered in the initial questionnaire included membership and attendance, staffing information, style or type of congregation, date the congregation was established, as well as length of time actively incorporating lay persons, programs, and activities provided, and space for additional comments.

Next the written data was collected and analyzed, and the interviews took place that fall. An overall total of forty usable responses were received; a substantial 69 percent of the fifty-eight recommended congregations. (Sixty-nine percent of the recommended congregations *is* a good rate of return on the survey. It is intriguing, however, that only 58 congregations—from a possible 7,433—were recommended by diocesan staff.)

Demographics

What types of congregations tend to have significant lay involvement? Are they congregations that have learned to manage the "Focus of Ministry" polarity well? Is overall involvement tied to living in authentic relationship with God [**M+**], supported by an organized Christian community [**E+**], and accordingly balanced and guided by the Baptismal Covenant? From the information provided by the congregations and the comments included with the diocesan recommendations, it was clear that there is quite a range of possibilities for why a particular congregation would have a significantly active or growing lay population. Episcopal congregations at times have been viewed as successful if they are growing, efficient, organized, or affluent [**E**]. Growth in membership and attendance does not necessarily indicate significant incorporation into a Christian community with involvement in living out the Baptismal covenant, but instead may indicate a dynamic, comforting, or entertaining clergy leader. In some cases the recommending diocesan officials stated that they were unsure of what was meant by a congregation with significant lay involvement and simply offered their recommendations based on their own sense of a successful congregation. (See appendix 1 for a sample of diocesan comments.)

Obviously, the small, family-size congregation requires a very high percentage of active Christians simply to maintain basic services for its members. This is especially noticeable when the congregation is too poor to hire a full-time priest. Thirty percent of the congregations studied were family-size. But another occasion for more active involvement occurs during the transition from a pastoral-size congregation to a program-size parish. This transition calls for more members to take on roles that had been expected of the clergy in the smaller, pastorally oriented congregation. Thirty-five percent of the congregations in this study were either transitioning from pastoral-size to program-size or were already functioning as program-size congregations.[1]

Overall, the forty congregations that were studied represented a cross section of demographic neighborhoods: 28.2 percent were suburban, 18.0 percent rural, 15.4 percent small town, 15.4 percent urban, 12.8 percent mixed communities, 5.1 percent inner city, and 5.1 percent university town.

Figure 2. Neighborhood Demographics

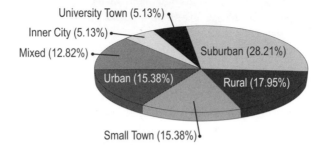

University Town (5.13%)
Inner City (5.13%)
Mixed (12.82%)
Suburban (28.21%)
Urban (15.38%)
Rural (17.95%)
Small Town (15.38%)

A broad cross-section of representatives was interviewed. Of those interviewed, 53.7 percent were ordained and 46.4 percent were not ordained. Fifty-five percent of those interviewed were male, while 45 percent were female. Eight of the congregations studied (20%) were what had been referred to as Canon 9 congregations with locally trained clergy, and an additional three congregations used both seminary-trained and local clergy.

At the time of the interviews, the Episcopal Church allowed in its constitution for locally trained clergy (referred to as "Canon 9") in cases where it might be difficult to hire and sustain seminary trained or "Canon 7" clergy. Canon 9 read in part: ". . . with regard to Dioceses with Congregations or missionary opportunities in communities which are small, isolated, remote, or distinct in respect of ethnic composition, language, or culture, and which cannot be provided sufficiently with the sacraments and pastoral ministrations of the Church through Clergy ordained under the provisions of Canon III.7, it shall be permissible . . . to establish procedures by which persons may be called by their Congregations and the Bishop with the Standing Committee, to be ordained local Priests and Deacons and licensed to serve the Congregations or communities out of which they were called."[2] In 2003, however, the Episcopal General Convention approved a reworking of the canons that refer to ministry. The old Canon 9 and its reference to "local priests and deacons" was one of the canons that was, in fact, deleted. The new canons do not assume a seminary education. The new Title III, Canon 8, "Of the Ordination of Priests," Section 4 addresses formation: "Postulants shall pursue the program of preparation for ordination to the Priesthood developed by the Bishop and Commission. The program shall include theological training, practical experience, emotional development, and spiritual formation. . . . Prior education and learning from life experience may be considered as part of the formation required for Priesthood. Whenever possible, formation for the Priesthood shall take place in community, including other persons in preparation for the Priesthood, a ministry team, or others preparing for ministry. . . ."[3]

Figure 3. Member Type Interviewed

Member Type Interviewed	Number Interviewed	Percent
Missioner	1	2.4%
Canon 9 priest	4	9.8%
Ministry team member	2	4.9%
Rector	12	29.3%
Associate priest	1	2.4%
Vicar	2	4.9%
Deacon	2	4.9%
Other staff	7	17.1%
Senior warden	8	19.5%
Other member	2	4.9%
Totals	**41**	**100.1%**

Congregational Size

The following chart illustrates the various sizes of the congregations recommended for this study, as well as of those actually interviewed. Size was based on the average Sunday attendance and interviewee comments regarding transitional phases.[4]

Figure 4. Congregational Size

Congregation Size	Percent Recommended	Percent Studied
Family (0-50)	24.0%	30.0%
Transitional Family/Pastoral	4.0%	5.0%
Pastoral (50-150)	14.0%	15.0%
Transitional Pastoral/Program	4.0%	2.5%
Program (150-350)	36.0%	32.5%
Transitional (Program/Corporate)	6.0%	7.5%
Corporation (350-500+)	12.0%	7.5%
Totals	**100%**	**100%**

There was no correlation between the number of years a congregation was actively promoting lay involvement and the percent of active members. This was true both when including the family-size congregations and when eliminating them, because the high percentage of involvement may have been due to the small actual number of members. Twenty percent of the congregations that were studied had actually been targeting lay involvement before the 1979 Book of Common Prayer's emphasis on baptismal covenant.

Percent Active

Each congregation was asked what percentage of the average Sunday attendance was active either in church activities or in Christian activities outside of church, beyond attendance at Sunday service. Because the "percent active" was based on the average Sunday attendance rather than church membership, it was possible to have results greater than 100 percent, especially in the smallest congregations. For example, if a small church has twenty-five members, but an average attendance of twelve (perhaps low due to work schedules or health issues), and fifteen were actively involved in ministry, the percent active was 125 percent.

Analysis of the percent of the congregation's members who were active, however, could not be used as the standard measure for this study because of too many extenuating variables. We have already seen that in some cases using this formula could result in higher than expected percentages when the Sunday attendance, for whatever reasons, was low. In the following actual response, I have underlined some unresolved phrases that illustrate additional possible issues:

> Let's count it up: choir 45; lay Eucharistic ministers, 4; acolytes/ servers, 4; ushers, 4; after-school enrichment volunteers, 12; monthly community breakfast cooks/servers, 30; support of single parent family, 4; foreign children's friendship project, 10; youth ministry leaders, 10; church school teachers, 11; Vestry and officers, 16 = 150. There are duplicates in this list (people involved in more than one project), but it ignores people who give time, leadership, or financial support on a project-by-project basis. In sharing these numbers with staff they believe I have still underestimated the involved numbers. So I think we can conservatively say that half of the regular worshipers are somehow involved beyond just the worship experience. The number involved in the community in programs not specifically emanating from the church would raise the percentage considerably.

Many family-size congregations indicated that they felt they lacked the critical mass necessary to be a fully functioning church even when 100 percent of its membership was actively involved. Active involvement in some of these cases resulted, not because lay involvement was specifically valued, but simply because there was no priest present. Adele Cerny commented that their congregation is so small that "*everyone* has to do *something*."[5] In *Total Ministry: Reclaiming the Ministry of All God's People*, Stewart C. Zabriskie offered a solution to this sometimes unrealistic expectation to live up to the demands of being what is perceived as a "fully functioning church": "We encourage congregations to reexamine the claims the church has in former times visited upon local parishes, usually with midsized and larger congregations seen as the norm. . . . We ask each local parish to pray about and consider what its vocation is *in the community where the parish is called to be unique*. . . . They do not spend a lot of time in church maintaining old functions. They *are* church where they live."[6]

Program-size congregations with newly engaged "lay leaders" were enthusiastic about their roles of leadership. In congregations of this size, however, there was not necessarily a sense that *each* member needed to make a contribution or had spiritual gifts to offer, only that more leaders were necessary and were becoming active. But an interesting phenomenon is that there may be a tendency to underestimate the number of active persons in a congregation of any size. And this tendency also may account for the low percentage of congregations recommended for this study. Some interviewees, including clergy, staff, and other members, gave a percent of their attendees who were active; then, upon reflection, the interviewee realized either by counting or by calculation that the percentage was indeed higher than their initial impression. A few congregations had realized this tendency to underestimate even before the interview. One congregation reported that they had been wondering why people were not becoming involved in a new program offered at the church. One of the staff members went through the parish directory noting which persons were already involved in other church activities. The realization was that most people were already committed to various church activities and, as another interviewee noted, it is hard to get over-committed people to come out for one more activity. Maintaining a database helps keep track of involved people. That is how Roberta Wexler knew that 113 percent[7] of the average 400 attendees at St. John's in Barrington, RI, were involved and therefore could be easily recognized during National Volunteer Month.[8] The realization on the part of the staff that their members are actively involved and dedicated, either inside the church or with other activities, and are not simply passive souls to be taken care of, is a healthy sign. This emerging awareness is a movement toward acknowledging that each Christian has a service or ministry to offer to God and their community. "This priesthood belongs to everyone. Every human being has some access to arcana that is given to no one else—at least, not in quite the same way. Every human being has a unique privilege of encounter with these arcana and therefore a unique priesthood. Everyone has a vocation leading them into a deeper acquaintance with God and so bringing them home to our true humanity in God's presence."[9] Indeed, priesthood is one of the primary elements of the covenant of baptism.

> We receive you into the household of God. Confess the faith of Christ crucified, proclaim his resurrection, and share with us in his eternal priesthood.
> (BCP, 308)

Questions for Reflection

1. Is your congregation type represented in this study?
2. What percentage of your members is active as Christians
   (a) inside the congregation's community life,
   (b) at work and/or at home,
   (c) in the local community,
   (d) in other aspects of the world and God's creation?

CHAPTER 5

Do You Believe?

Grace St. Paul's parish became a worshiping community as a merged congregation formed out of two independent parishes. The bishop first proposed a merger between the two congregations after a fiscal crisis at Grace Church; the idea was accepted later after the city had undertaken a protracted period of road work in front of St. Paul's building that made the parish all but inaccessible for over a year.

Discussions began with a combined meeting of the two vestries followed by a joint Sunday worship service. Parishioners filled the pews, a powerful sermon called all to a spirit of unity, and the baptism of a child added to the moment. Official Vestry actions in both parishes formed a Merger Committee. Meetings often happened over breakfast and usually included a celebration of the holy Eucharist. Individual subcommittees dealt with finance, parish programs, worship and liturgics, staff and administration, buildings and grounds, and corporate and legal matters.

"We are a community centered in prayer and sacrament. All ministry grows out of our experience of corporate worship and individual spiritual growth. This ministry is expressed in parish outreach and evangelism, and by individual Christians in their daily life and work.

"It is the particular vision of this merger that, as a result of the combination of Grace and St. Paul's parishes, a comprehensive parish will be created that will be spiritually and financially stronger, can lead in evangelism and will be able to serve in full the diversity of Episcopalians in [this area].

Opportunities for worship, spiritual growth, fellowship, pastoral care, outreach and education in the Christian faith will be provided for persons of all ages; this implies a continuation of programs that exist and a new emphasis on offerings especially for children, youth and families. The new parish with its increased strength and financial and human resources will also help provide leadership for the Episcopal Church." [Statement of Vision]

As a central feature, the merger proposal created a new parish. It named St. Paul's rector as the first rector of the parish and Grace's warden as its first Senior Warden. The new parish home was to be located on the site of the former Grace Church. There still remained the legal, human, and spiritual effort to make the merger a reality and not just a dream. That reality began with a procession on Palm Sunday from the secularized St. Paul's building to the newly designated Grace St. Paul's; it was an exciting and moving experience that involved nearly four hundred people. As the procession walked along, the sound of St. Paul's former church bell could be heard tolling from atop Grace St. Paul's building. Parishioners soon settled into the sanctuary of the "new" church, adopting a worship style that both emerged from the traditions of the two previous parishes and grew in the context of the new one. Eventually the stained glass windows from St. Paul's building were installed in the clerestory of the merged church. The rebuilding of the old Grace Church organ incorporated many of the re-voiced pipes from the St. Paul's organ. The sale of the St. Paul's property marked the final resettling of the former St. Paul's congregation into its new location and was the final step of the physical aspects of the merger. Money from the sale gave the congregation the financial breathing space it needed to get on its feet and expand its programs.

With the addition of new members who had belonged neither to Grace nor St. Paul's, a third segment of the "people of Grace St. Paul's" soon came into existence. This growing part of the parish infused the community's life with new energy and fresh perspectives. The future is bright for Grace St.

Paul's. *It is blessed with growing numbers of fine people, a dedicated staff of paid and volunteer workers, beautiful and creative worship, a fine physical plant, many strong programs, a progressive theology, and a measure of financial security. It is also an example of the Christian ideal of community, formed out of struggle and faith, and focused on the Good News of Jesus Christ.* [1]

Do you believe in God the Father?
Do you believe in Jesus Christ the Son of God?
Do you believe in God the Holy Spirit?
(BCP, 304)

In terms of the action of God, Baptism signifies and imparts the outreaching love of the Father, restoring persons to relation with himself. It unites persons with Christ the Redeemer, and places them with the redemption-bearing community, his Body. It is the seal in the Holy Spirit of the new life, present and to come. In terms of the human response, Baptism enacts and shapes the entry on the life of faith, obedience and expectation. It is the sacrament of conversion, expressing a new mind, a re-direction, the rejection of the tyranny of sin and the commitment to righteousness. It is the inauguration of a life renewed and set free. All of Christian life—its beginnings and its end, now and forever—is related to the life of God in a bond that is not broken. [2]

Do you believe . . . ? Yes. Yes, of course, it goes without saying. Indeed, often it is *not* said. Fifty percent of those interviewed made no reference to God in the course of the interview, nor were such references made in their printed materials such as newsletters and welcoming brochures. In the 50 percent of the congregations who did talk about God and the importance of prayer and Scripture study during the interviews, however, all referenced such items in their written works. Understandably, there may be some reluctance to using a language that has been co-opted by the TV evangelists and others in order to "sell their product" [E-], however, these 50 percent were able to make references to the importance of God in their lives and such relationships in a sincere and open manner.

Those who did not talk about a relational God focused instead, both in their literature and in conversation, on themes of survival, ministry, and service activities, plans and programs, and community building. Carlyle Fielding Stewart has also noticed this phenomenon: "In many mainline liberal Protestant denominations there appears to be a culture of disdain or contempt for using the language of spirituality and a culture of holiness as a basis for spiritual interaction and empowerment. . . . This was also true of our regional church meetings and gatherings. Any mention of the Holy Spirit to guide the judgment, direction, and renewal of the church was sternly rebuked."[3]

There was somewhat of a correlation between clergy or those with theological training being more likely to talk about God. The occurrences, however, were generally mixed. In addition, since the printed materials of the congregation reflected the language of the interviewee, it appears that referring to God or not referring to God was a phenomenon of the congregation as an entity, rather than of the particular respondent. This can be accounted for in that congregations who talk about God are more likely to call a rector who is comfortable with that language, just as communities who are not used to this personal reference to God may be uncomfortable with a candidate who would talk about Jesus and the importance of spiritual disciplines during the search process. In A. Wayne Schwab's *When the Members Are the Missionaries: An Extraordinary Calling for Ordinary People,* Kevin states: "Most of us do not know how to talk about what we believe in . . . . If you are unsure of something, you do not talk about it much. My belief came through no sudden revelation. It came over time. It came from working with people who have similar faith and similar thoughts. Wherever you go, you can meet people with solid conviction. Yes, I probably do seek them out."[4]

Figure 5. God Talk by Role of Interviewee

God Talk by Role	reference to God	no reference to God
Regular clergy	11	4
Staff	3	4
Parishioner	1	6
Canon 9 team & congregation	5	6
TOTALS	20	20

Average attendance and congregational size were not related to which communities used faith verbalization. Nor was there a correlation between the congregation's reported percent active and the verbalization of faith. The average percent active for those who did not verbalize a faith relationship was 60.4 percent while those who did verbalize a faith relationship was 63.2 percent. (The calculation for "percent active" compared to "faith verbalization" was performed without the family-sized congregations due to the problems with the "critical mass" skew.) Neither was there a correlation between the use of faith language and whether the motivating factor for increased lay involvement came from the minister, the people, or money issues; 50 percent of each set used faith language. There was no correlation between the number of years of lay involvement and a congregation's use of faith language; so it did not appear to be something that develops naturally over time, nor something present at first that then declines.

In terms of neighborhood types, most categories showed a near 50 percent use of verbalization; the lowest being 27 percent for suburban communities.[5] Rural areas were 43 percent, small towns, inner city, and university towns all were 50 percent, and urban neighborhoods were 66 percent. Of the congregations studied, however, of those who described their areas as mixed, 80 percent used faith verbalization. This higher percentage may reflect a congregation's clearer focus for its existence due to its participation in, and experience of, a larger cross section of God's kingdom. The basic human experiences of God's covenant love and striving for a faithful response may give the members a common language with which they can communicate. Biblical references can illustrate this experience: "Amazed and astonished, they asked, 'Are not all these who are speaking Galileans? And how is it that we hear, each of us, in our own native language? Parthians, Medes, Elamites, . . . —in our own languages we hear them speaking about God's deeds of power'" (Acts 2:7–12); and ". . . in Christ Jesus you are all children of God through faith. As many of you as were baptized into Christ have clothed yourselves with Christ. There is so longer Jew or Greek, there is no longer slave or free, there is no longer male or female; for all of you are one in Christ Jesus" (Galatians 3:26–28).

Figure 6. Percent Faith Verbalization by Neighborhood Type

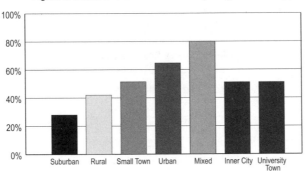

Figure 7. Comparison Between Faith Verbalization & Financial Stability

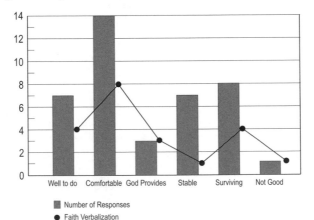

44

Figure 8. Role of Priest

Role of Priest / Faith Language	Total
sacraments icon	19
building Body	13
equip others	12
administrator	23
wisdom	7
patron	0
contributor	1
assistance	1
faith	4
Mighty deeds	1
tongues	0
prophecy	0
discernment	1
Own gifts	1
pastor	11
service	2
healing	0
compassion	8
knowledge	4
teacher	8
exhort/urge	8
evangelist	2
apostle-sent	1

Column (respondent) headers: 1, 35, 8, 4, 5, 7, 14, 11, 31, 28, 33, 16, 29, 3, 32, 38, 34, 12, 2, 39, 40, 6, 21, 24, 13, 36, 17, 9, 20, 10, 22, 23, 18, 25, 26, 27, 30, 37, 15, 19 — (Faith Language total: 20)

In comparing financial stability with the use of faith verbalization, half of those congregations who were well to do (57%), comfortable (57%), or surviving (50%) used such language. Poor but stable congregations had a much lower rate (14%). Although the sample size is small, 100 percent of both the congregations who either said that God provides for their needs or said that they were just not doing well at all financially used faith language.

The sample size of congregations employing both seminary-trained and locally trained clergy (three congregations) may be too small to be definitive, but 100 percent of these congregations verbalized their faith in God, while only 55 percent of the congregations headed solely by seminary-trained clergy and 40 percent of the Canon 9 local clergy did likewise.

In looking at the role of the priest and comparing those congregations who used faith and biblical language to those who did not, several tendencies are apparent. Although both groups equally described the priest as sacramentalist and administrator, the faith language group more often expected the priest to have the gift of wisdom or be a vision setter. The priests in congregations employing faith language were described as equipping others and building the Body of Christ more often. Other gifts, such as faith, miraculous works, and discernment, as well as recognizing that the priest was a person with his or her own specific gifts, were mentioned solely by the faith language group. The gifts of pastoral care were more frequently referred to by those who did not use faith language. Teaching activities were mentioned by both groups, although the gift of knowledge was listed more by the non-faith language group, and the gift of exhortation more by the faith language group.

There was an interesting negative correlation to note: A very high percentage of the congregations in this particular short study that replied "yes, we do political, social justice ministry" were ones who did *not* obviously use faith language, while, of those who did use faith language, half replied "some" social justice issues were raised, and the other half replied "no," "minimal," "raise it in quiet ways," or "stance of the individual." Perhaps this counter-connection in the overtly active group is due to the shift in focus toward the power and control issues prevalent in institutional, political, and justice systems [**E**] with attention being drawn away from the aspect of God's power, that of loving-mercy, grace, and kindness [**M**]. Special attention to the balance of the Focus of Ministry Polarity will need to be maintained when grappling with this area. For although the original focus of the congregation's social justice efforts may be based within God's loving realm, when fighting with social entities that value power and control, there is a very real danger in buying into their viewpoint in order to fight on the same turf.

The inner struggle for Christians regarding social justice is one of being in the world but not of it. Christians are confronted with obvious injustice that they feel surely can't be God's will, but they have also heard the message of love for enemies and forgiveness: "Love your enemies, do good to those who hate you, bless those who curse you, pray for those who abuse you" (Luke 6:27–38). The result is often uncertainty and therefore inaction on the part of churchgoers. Mary Ann Hinsdale, in *It Comes from the People: Community Development and Local Theology*, reports: "Faith and religious convictions [are] concepts that are often suspect in community organizing circles, since they are seen as dulling and prohibitive to the development process."[6]

Further, convincing downtrodden people to acknowledge their own power and act on it, in order to combat the oppressive systems that attempt to dominate them, could result in an abandonment of the faith they have: If God won't help us through this predicament, we'll just have to do it ourselves. Ed Chambers, as director of the Industrial Areas Foundation, is quoted in *Cold Anger: A Story of Faith and Power Politics* as stating, "We are trained to give consent to people in authority. . . . But when you become mature, when you are informed, when you know yourself, you begin to take responsibility for your own actions and you begin to make decisions about when you will and will not consent to someone else's power."[7] Allowing people to recognize their situation and accept their own power, instead of giving it away to those in authority, is the energy that community organization efforts try to tap. The danger for Christians would be taking upon oneself the responsibility, power, and authority that in fact belong to God alone. And so Chambers further clarifies his thoughts: "Some in religion may call it spirit—the holy spirit. But I call it power. God gave us this power over our lives. It is a gift, and we shouldn't give it away to others."[8]

The balanced goal in Christian social justice efforts would be one of discerning God's will and methods through study of the issues, Scripture reading, and prayer [M+], and then standing alongside one's Lord in the organized battle against evil [E+]. Jesus prays for his disciples: "I am not asking you to take them out of the world, but I ask you to protect them from the evil one. They do not belong to the world, just as I do not belong to the world. . . . As you have sent me into the world, so I have sent them into the world. And for their sakes I sanctify myself, so that they also may be sanctified in truth" (John 17:15–19).

Although expressions of faith can show up anywhere, and in fact did occur in each type of setting, faith verbalization appeared most commonly when there was significant diversity among the congregation's members and/or staff. At one congregation in the southwest, not only do they use faith language, but the turning point for lay involvement came "due to an English-speaking rector [being] called to serve a mostly non-English-speaking congregation. Therefore, many lay people had to get involved in the daily operations." Both mixed neighborhoods and those congregations with a combination of seminary-trained clergy and locally trained clergy had a significantly high percentage of faith verbalization. This correlation does not necessarily provide a blueprint for action since several causal antecedents, or a combination of factors, are possible. For instance, when these groups that contained members of significantly differing backgrounds were formed, perhaps they found common ground most fruitfully in their common relationship with God, resulting in a community using the language of faith. Equally possible, though, was that as these communities became strong in their faith, and shared their experiences of God, they then became open enough to allow for a diverse congregation and/or staff—indeed, even to strive for it. Letty Russell comments:

> We know that commitment is more likely to grow where there is responsibility, vulnerability, equality, and trust among those who share a diversity of gifts and resources. Because partnerships are living relationships that share the "already/not yet" character of new creation, they are always in process and never finished, as they draw us together in common struggle and work, involving risk, continuing growth, and hopefulness in moving toward a goal or purpose transcending the group. By definition, partnership involves growing interdependence in relation to God, persons and creation so that we are constantly in interaction with a wider community of persons, social structures, values, and beliefs that may provide support, correctives, or negative feedback. There is never complete equality in such a dynamic relationship, but a pattern of equal regard and mutual acceptance of different gifts among partners is essential.[9]

This leads to the next question: "What was the original turning point, motivation, or deciding factor for significant involvement in each of these congregations?"

Typically some type of excitement is required to generate the energy that is needed to move the people of a congregation out of a maintenance mode [E-].[10] Seventy-nine percent of the fourteen family-sized congregations indicated financial issues. Many of those congregations who were unable to afford a seminary-trained priest reported either doing the work themselves, or having turned to "total ministry" or "mutual ministry," using locally trained members in order to solve their dilemma. Seventy-seven percent of the congregations who have been working with locally trained, non-stipendiary Canon 9 clergy report that they were now stable in terms of finances. A few of these congregations indicated

Figure 9. Motivation for Lay Involvement

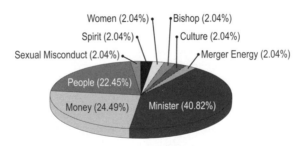

during the interview that they would like to save up for a seminary-trained priest. This response is not surprising, Stewart Zabriskie reflected: "Many small congregations are still mourning the loss of a ministry model that is no longer appropriate. They lose their sense of baptismal vocation in recurring waves of nostalgia. . . . While it is difficult to document this nostalgic mood statistically, it is part of the pulse of a place: the deeply rooted reluctances, humilities, strengths, and memories that are so much of a congregation's personality."[11] Only one *non*-family-sized congregation listed money as a motivator. Additional motivators mentioned for family-sized congregations included: the minister, the bishop, the people, and clergy sexual misconduct.

In all, the greatest deciding factor reported for increased lay involvement was a clergy person who encouraged it (40.8%). Financial issues overall accounted for 24.5 percent of the congregations studied. The congregations motivated by financial reasons, generally because they were the family-sized congregations, had the highest level of active members, averaging 79.4 percent. The parishioners themselves called for increased involvement in 22.5 percent of the cases. It is interesting to observe, though, that when studying just the larger congregations, the ones whose motivation came from the members themselves had a higher average of active members (71.2%) than those congregations whose lay involvement impetus came from the clergy (58.8%). One congregation received its energy for renewal when two previously separate congregations were merged into one body. One congregation specifically reported the spirit of renewal and the Holy Spirit's involvement as the causal factor for increased involvement of its members.

Why did the people get involved? One interviewee spelled out the question: "What does it take to become aware, to sit up and take notice, after God may have been taken for granted for so long? We can be like fish in the sea discussing whether water exists" until God breaks through in some type of sacramental moment.[12] Another interviewee described her congregation's motivation by explaining that the people did not realize how much the church meant to them until there was a fire. "The stained glass window of the dove didn't get broken, so we felt that the Holy Spirit was still with us. The people are more involved now." Still another summarized their experience as follows: "The people are baptized for ministry and then confirmation strengthens, empowers and sustains them. But it really takes a conversion, a change in mind-set from a consumer mind-set, to an expectation of participation."[13] The merger of two congregations, financial difficulties, and sexual misconduct are all opportunities for reassessment, refocusing, and being open to the Spirit. Robert Greenleaf, in *Servant Leadership: A Journey into the Nature of Legitimate Power and Greatness*, writes about times when "*all is confusion.*" This "presents an opportunity because it *is* a threat. . . . Many able leaders . . . feel that a prolonged period of calm and stability is a greater threat to viability than is an occasional state of confusion. So, when appropriate, they will do something deliberately to create confusion—not so much that the institution founders, but enough that it will be challenged to new life."[14]

Even in the normal course of life these opportunities arise. "Every now and then, life forces us to ask one of the questions that we've been avoiding. Something happens that jolts us loose from our comfortable oblivion. . . . We arrive at a new stage of life and find that our former ways of coping no longer work. Then, if we let ourselves look honestly at what is happening, God begins showing us surprising answers to our questions."[15] The church recognizes several opportunities for reorganization at key moments in life with specific church ceremonies or ritual prayers. These are instances when the church's historic and communal experience of God [E+] is called upon to help an individual interpret the message and revelation of God for oneself [M+]. Once introduced to God in this way, it becomes easier to recognize and understand God's action throughout life. But such understanding doesn't happen automatically: it often takes much practice, but then it becomes second nature. Just as the secret of learning to read begins with knowing the letters and then recognizing emerging patterns, eventually one can't help but automatically notice God's actions and translate God's meaning at a glance. And yet there is an important distinction in being read *to* and in knowing how to read by oneself:

> The deepest arcana are secret because they are hard to know, hard to reveal, hard to learn. They can be known only by experiencing them. Anything that can be fully conveyed in language, without remainder, is probably not of ultimate importance. . . . Some things are known only through our direct involvement. You cannot know what it is to be in love until it happens to you. You cannot know what it is to stand, unprotected, in GOD's presence until you are there.[16]

Questions for Reflection

1. What do you believe "about" God? (Knowledge)
2. Do you believe "in" God? (Faith)

If so, does your behavior reflect your belief? If so, describe. If not, explain.

3. Do you believe God? (Intimate knowledge and experience)

What do you believe God is telling you? Is this something you want to believe?
How does this effect your actions?

After answering the questions first for yourself, describe the image your congregation as a body seems to reflect regarding each.

CHAPTER 6

The Church

In the science fiction book, *A Canticle for Leibowitz*, Walter M. Miller, Jr. depicts what happens when purpose and meaning [M] are lost from the "Focus of Ministry" balance and all that remains is church organization and structure [E]. Although written in the 1950s, and telling a story about the future church after a nuclear holocaust, parallels can be seen to both the past and the present:

> If the old drawings were worth saving at all, they needed to be recopied every century or two anyhow. Not only did the original copies fade, but often the redrawn versions became nearly illegible after a time, due to the impermanence of the inks employed.
>
> ... He studied it until he could see the whole amazing complexity with his eyes closed, but knew no more than he had known before. ... It made so little sense that a long period of staring at it produced a stupefying effect. Nevertheless he began work at duplicating every detail, even to the copying of a central brownish stain which he thought might be the blood of the Blessed Martyr, but which Brother Jeris suggested was only the stain left by a decayed apple core.
>
> ... "But now the creature-diagram itself represents something, does it not? What does the diagram represent?" ...
>
> Francis reddened, "I would imagine," he said slowly, after pausing to stifle his annoyance, "that the diagram represents an abstract concept, rather than a concrete thing. Perhaps the ancients had a systematic method for depicting a pure thought. It's clearly not a recognizable picture of an object."
>
> "Yes, yes, it's clearly *un*recognizable!" Brother Jeris agreed with a chuckle.
>
> "On the other hand, perhaps it does depict an object, but only in a very formal stylistic way—so that one would need special training or—"
>
> "Special eyesight?"
>
> "In my opinion, it's a high abstraction of perhaps transcendental

value expressing a thought of the Beatus Leibowitz."

"Bravo! Now what was he thinking about?"

. . . He dared change nothing that he did not understand, but surely the parts tables and the block-lettered information could be spread symmetrically around the diagram on scrolls and shields. Because the meaning of the diagram itself was obscure, he dared not alter its shape or plan by a hair; but since its color scheme was unimportant, it might as well be beautiful. . . . The general shape, over-all, with a scrolled border, might well become a shield, rather than the stark rectangle which enclosed the drawing in the print. He made dozens of preliminary sketches. At the very top of the parchment would be a representation of the Triune God, and at the very bottom—the coat of arms of the Albertian Order, with, just above it the image of the Beatus.

. . .[much later]

Brother Librarian groaned as yet another lead-sealed cask was rolled out of storage for unsealing. Armbruster was not impressed by the fact that the secular scholar, in two days, had unraveled a bit of a puzzle that had been lying around, a complete enigma, for a dozen centuries. To the custodian of the Memorabilia, each unsealing represented another decrease in the probable lifetime of the contents of the cask, and he made no attempt to conceal his disapproval of the entire proceeding. To Brother Librarian, whose task in life was the preservation of books, the principal reason for the existence of books was that they might be preserved perpetually. Usage was secondary, and to be avoided if it threatened longevity.[1]

I believe in . . . the holy catholic Church
(BCP, 304)

The first-century Christians organized themselves into a recognizable structured format [E+]:

They devoted themselves to the apostles' teaching and fellowship, to the breaking of bread and the prayers. Awe came upon everyone, because many wonders and signs were being done by the apostles. All who believed were together and had all things in common; they would sell their possessions and goods and distribute the proceeds to all, as any had need. Day by day, as they spent much time together in the temple, they broke bread at home and ate their food with glad and generous hearts, praising God and having the goodwill of all the people. And day by day the Lord added to their number those who were being saved. (Acts 2:42–47)

Before long, however, the newly formed church began to encounter the negative aspects of the institutional side of the Focus of Ministry polarity. Verna Dozier reflects: "The ancient Hebrews, during the time of their establishment as a nation among other nations, distorted the call by turning it into law. The Christians, during the time of their becoming a structure among other structures of the world, distorted the call by turning it into institution."[2] The book of Revelation begins with an account of the church's sinful actions [E-] and God's invitation for a renewed relationship with the church and its members over a covenantal meal— and it's back to square one [M+]. The following summarizes what was written to the messengers of the early churches:

> These are the words of the Son of God . . . I know your works, I know your affliction . . . But I have this against you . . . You have abandoned the love you had at first. . . . I have not found your works [complete] in the sight of my God . . . you are neither cold nor hot . . . I reprove and discipline those whom I love. Be earnest, therefore, and repent. Listen! I am standing at the door, knocking; if you hear my voice and open the door, I will come in to you and eat with you, and you with me. . . .
> Let anyone who has an ear listen to what the Spirit is saying to the churches.
> (See Revelation 2:1–3:22)

The Christian community has recognized many valuable, sacred components both in the movements of the past and in more recent experiences [M+]. In order not to lose these many and varied experiences, the church attempts to organize, clarify, preserve, and maintain them [E+]. One interviewee exemplifies this since he was from a charismatic congregation [M+] that was looking to add some order [E+] to help balance the organizational aspects. His spoken concern was how that structure could be helpful without being oppressive [E-].[3]

"Our fundamental task, as the church, is to create a culture, ethos, or environment [E] where the people of God can grow spiritually in the Word, in service and witness to the congregation and community, and in every area of their lives" [M+].[4] But it is difficult to contain an experience of God and an ongoing relationship with the Holy Spirit solely in an institutional package. And so David J. Bosch in *Transforming Mission: Paradigm Shifts in Theology of Mission* comments:

> Our main point of censure should . . . not be that the movement became an institution but that, when this happened, it also lost much of its verve. Its white-hot convictions, poured into the hearts of the first adherents, cooled down and became crystallized codes, solidified institutions, and petrified dogmas. The prophet became a priest of the establishment, charisma became office, and love became routine. The horizon was no longer the world but the boundaries of the local parish. The impetuous missionary torrent of earlier years was tamed into a still-flowing rivulet and eventually

into a stationary pond. It is this development that we have to deplore.[5]

Is the church community today more like the Body of Christ or a business organization with the sacred as the commodity? Does baptism signify a reaffirmation of one's place in God's family, or is it more like joining a social club, one with educational opportunities, a chance to be elected or chosen for an office, or perhaps employed as a director, with the availability of stock options? Does the church act like it is marketing products or helping to build loving relationships with God and neighbor?

One business tool that actually may be able to assist Christian congregations to acknowledge and articulate their experience of God is the mission or vision statement. "Visions inherently raise expectations about the future, help people invest in the future, consolidate interests, promulgate and solidify values, energize people, galvanize cooperative networks essential to community and faith building, and enable people to share their faith and beliefs by building community around common ideals."[6]

Many of the congregations studied published vision or mission statements in their printed literature. Some of these statements spoke eloquently of such elements as the Baptismal Covenant, the Trinity, mission, and faith; these were recorded as part of the field notes. It became apparent, however, that these statements did not always accurately reflect the day-to-day operations in many of the congregations. At times when a congregation's statement appeared particularly significant in terms of lay involvement and was referred to by the interviewer in an attempt to clarify its relevance, the interviewee was unfamiliar with the content of the statement. Comments such as "That's old, we don't refer to it," were received during the interviews. Also, when a statement was not included with the information packet, and it was requested from the interviewee, the response often was that they knew they had one, did not know what it was, but they could find it if the interviewer needed it. Although these type of statements did exist on paper, their original purpose, that of providing a spiritual vision for action and mission, was no longer being fulfilled. Roy Oswald and Robert Friedrich have found: "In a congregation that has been around for twenty to eighty years or more, that common vision is long gone. What usually takes its place is the dream that they might serve their own members more fully."[7]

Several congregations did know and referred to their statements during the course of the interview. In general, though, the congregation's official summary statements did not provide a consistent element by which to determine the theologies, or even the lived visions, of the recommended congregations that were studied. Verna Dozier and Celia Hahn, too, were aware of this type of mixed message when they wrote: "Note that I am making a distinction between what many people honestly believe they believe in their hearts and what they *do* corporately in the institution. . . . The leaders of the church do talk and try to believe the grace game. But they *play* the law game. There's the rub—the difference between religion of the lips and religion of action."[8]

Effective organizations, however, do require meaningful and inspiring visions in order to function. It is shown throughout the Hebrew Scriptures that "the vision of Israel's greatness did not simply grow out of the minds of the people, but was cultivated in their covenantal relationship. Because they had a viable relationship with Yahweh, they knew that Yahweh had great expectations and high hopes for them."[9] William Countryman also describes this ultimate goal:

> The great purpose of human existence is to enjoy communion with GOD and with GOD 's creation. . . . "You shall love the LORD your GOD with all your heart and with all your life and with all your understanding and with all your strength" and "You shall love your neighbor as yourself" (Mark 12:28–31). These are not merely commandments or rules, but a portrayal of the richest and most joyous kind of human life, the existence we were made for from the beginning.
>
> This priestly existence, however, is not automatic. Like every human excellence, we have to practice it, reflect on it, and grow into it. . . . What we can do . . . is make ourselves open and available for the conversation with the TRANSCENDENT and with one another.[10]

Christian communities need to *consciously* strive for this intimate goal and live into it. "A congregation is 'designed' to get the results it is getting. If we do not change the vision of the congregation's purpose, we will continue to get what we have always gotten. If we embrace a new vision, we must redesign the congregation around it. Every member and every leader need to understand and do their part to realize the vision."[11]

Indeed, Oswald and Friedrich maintain that mission statements need to be reviewed and rewritten at least every four to five years since congregations change over time.[12] It is possible that without an updated focus statement, "an older congregation's members hold quite disparate views about what the mission of the congregation ought to be. Rather than holding a vision in common, they learn to live with each other, even though they have great difficulty agreeing on where the congregation ought to focus its energy."[13] This ongoing redefining of purpose and mission is like an examination of conscience. Caroline A. Westerhoff, in *Calling: A Song for the Baptized*, expresses this well: "We must heed two notes of warning, though. Clarity about aim does not mean that that aim is in concert with the reign of God. Demonic systems can produce great energy for survival and growth. Moreover, that which we espouse as purpose or mission and what we actually practice are never in absolute harmony. Indeed, they can be quite far apart. Our need to survive as a body always pollutes our practice to some degree. So we are to ask continually, 'What do we intend, and what is actually happening?'"[14]

To start the process of developing a statement, include the whole congregation. Without adequate buy-in there may indeed be goals to work on but not "a group of people on fire about a sense of mission they hold in common."[15] Next the congregation needs to discern their *real* purpose, not just what they say they do or what they think they're expected to do.[16] It is suggested that many elements be included in this process, such as the congregation's and denomination's history and traditions, individual experiences, cultural dynamics, local and community needs, as well as Scripture and prayer. "Most important though is the leadership and guidance of the Holy Spirit"[17] [E+ **through** M+]. This whole process can be an opportunity to develop a deeper level of maturity and a more intimate knowledge and experience of God, leading the members and congregation as a whole to a deeper commitment to Christ and Christian mission. Further, Oswald and Friedrich point out that much like a creed, mission statements reflect the congregation's beliefs and the resulting implications for action. They suggest that a mission statement can be and should be used as part of the liturgical rites as well as in the context of regular meetings. Such practices will help balance the Focus of Ministry polarity by using both strategic and spiritual terms to provide a focus on God's goals for the congregation. Like a positive, personal affirmation that is repeatedly recited, "a congregation that affirms an identity through a mission statement will over time actualize that vision."[18]

The baptismal covenant, too, is the specific statement of the Christian vision and direction for mission. It is an organizational list of guidelines and directives for fulfilling the Christian life [E+]. When accepted and reaffirmed often by God and the church community, the baptismal covenant has the potential to continue the acts of creation, redemption, and empowerment initiated and brought about by God's love [M+]. This reaffirmation is a renewal of the relationship with the Lord of the covenant, a love affair, a courtship, an ongoing comforting, yet challenging, relationship.[19]

Come, O Holy Spirit, come;
come as the wind and cleanse;
come as the fire and burn;
convict,
convert, and
consecrate
the minds and hearts of these your servants,
to their great good and to your great glory;
who with the Father and the Son are one God,
now and forever.
Amen.[20]

Questions for Reflection

1. The first chapter of Genesis describes God's power of moving chaos into order through creation. In applying the concept of polarity, the church's role can therefore be seen as providing order to the ongoing creation that God works through us. Some of the ways the church does this is by alerting its members to the dangers of self-centeredness and selfishness, and by refocusing on the Spirit's guidance to new life, so that the church's own need for stability does not stagnant into death.

Do you agree or disagree? Explain your answer.

2. Understanding that in today's culture of setting priorities what one does *first* is often the *only* thing that one has time for, what is the first priority for your church members? Is this the same priority for your church staff/clergy? Is this priority spoken of with a sense of urgency?

3. How might you re-address your congregation's basic *need* (building project, children's education, dwindling membership, internal conflicts, volunteer burnout), if you were to put the first priority on the development of a solid relationship with God?

CHAPTER 7

Will You Continue?

"How Has St. John's Touched Your Life? We're With You All The Way." This was a theme used to highlight the way our parishioners share their time, talent, and treasure with St. John's, the community, and the world. Some of the activities that we used to expand this subject were as follows:

We developed a colorful card that had a time line listed on the front of the card with important sacraments and activities: Baptism, Sunday School, Spiritual Life, Youth Group, Confirmation, Marriage, Adult Education, Loving Community, and Burial. The back of the card was filled with every ministry team, our annual events, that year's upcoming fellowship activities, our adult education classes, outreach activities and the names of the staff who support our lay ministries.

The Shared Ministry Team developed a slide show based on this card. A gifted parishioner took photos of dozens of St. John's members and designed a slide show utilizing both sides of the card. Photos identified different "ways" we were with an individual (baptism, confirmation, marriage, etc.), as well as different ministry teams in action (outreach activities, fellowship, adult education forums, etc.). The slide show was used as the sermon for all services that weekend.

In addition we asked our parishioners to write stories about their experiences at St. John's throughout their life here and published them in our monthly newsletter. These were remarkable stories of faith, community, and fellowship during times of joy and distress. It was a wonderful way for *people to share their lives while expressing how St. John's had been with them "all the way."*

We are blessed to have so many gifted people here at St. John's. There was great joy evidenced as a result of this project which highlighted how St. John's had touched the lives of so many people and that we truly were "with you all the way."

(Written by Bobbi Wexler, St. John's Episcopal Church, Barrington, Rhode Island[1])

Will you continue in the apostles' teaching and fellowship, in the breaking of the bread, and in the prayers?
(BCP, 304)

The crowd's response to Peter's first proclamation regarding Jesus' life, death, and resurrection at Pentecost as recorded in the Acts of the Apostles was that they were "cut to the heart" and wanted to know what they should do. His directions contain the give and take, calling, and response of relationship: "Repent, and be baptized every one of you in the name of Jesus Christ so that your sins may be forgiven; and you will receive the gift of the Holy Spirit" (Acts 2:38) [M+]. Just a few verses later is a description of the early church as institution: "They devoted themselves to the apostles' [trained leaders] teaching [set standards] and fellowship [organization], to the breaking of bread [ritual] and the prayers [a focus on God but through the institution's formula prayers]" (Acts 2:42) [E+]. These original organizational principles of the early Christian community are reiterated in the 1979 Episcopal baptismal ceremony as a key question in the covenant ritual. This one question alone is packed with many elements, each of which received devoted attention from the early congregations.

The Apostles' Teaching

"Christian education is education in Christ, and presupposes a certain relationship of the person who receives it to Christ. Eliminate that relationship and the education ceases at once to be Christian for him who receives it. . . . And so we gradually slip into the position of building on another foundation than Christ without being aware of it."[2] Thus, some churches today have slipped into the business model of offering educational programs much like products, the success of which are determined by the number of participants or customers. Often in these cases the primary questions become: What do the customers want? What new and improved courses should we offer? How can we get more people to attend? And important truths become cute advertising slogans [E-]. But the early apostles' teaching was in fact witnessing about how Jesus lived among them. Questions from the early disciples regarding their personal experiences, problems, and current life situations were answered with examples from the Scriptures, with guidance from the Holy Spirit through prayer, and with concrete instances of what Jesus actually did or said about those types of situations [M+]. As the early church grew, the "apostles' teaching" became summarized by the epistles or letters, the Gospels, and the creeds in an attempt to preserve the authentic message [E+]. Often this body of teaching was assembled specifically to assist new members in coming to know who Jesus was, in being introduced to God's loving forgiveness, and in receiving the Holy Spirit's power and gifts for life as a follower of Jesus—a Christian. The instruction was given in preparation to enter a covenant with God through baptism and the Eucharist. In some parts of the early Christian church, a lengthy preparatory catechumenate arose followed by mystagogia (teachings regarding mystical doctrines) as additional instruction after the baptism ceremony. The good news of Jesus was told, owned, and retold. Eventually, the personal oral accounts of Jesus and the apostles were written down for general use, as were letters of advice from various leaders to specific early Christian communities.

Today many churches rely on Christian education or formation programs to supply their members with the advice and guidance that is needed for living the Christian faith. In the congregations that were interviewed, a variety of services were offered to the membership in order to provide for ongoing education and support. Nearly all of the congregations (92%) offered some type of adult education; the ones who did not were family-sized who did not believe that they had the resources to offer it. (Some small congregations used diocesan resources or teamed up with neighboring parishes to offer programs.) Bible study was offered in 80 percent of the congregations. Several used the baptismal covenant as a basis for programs that were offered to newcomers as well as to ongoing members. These programs often addressed the basic expectations of the faith and how the commitment can be lived out. These congregations made references such as "Baptism brings people into the Kingdom and helps them grow, in baptism we are adopted into the priesthood of all." Liturgically based programs like the catechumenate emphasize both the seriousness of the Christian commitment and the supportive role of the congregation in preparing people for baptism.

Continuing Christian formation, especially Scripture study and sharing, are important for all Christians, no matter where they are in their life's journey. Wayne Schwab, in *When the Members Are the Missionaries*, details a Bible reflection group that differs from both an intellectual study and a discussion group. Highlights of this model include:

- What is said is addressed to the Holy Spirit.
- Questions are asked such as: "Where does this passage touch my life, my community, our nation, or our world?" "From what I have heard and shared, what does God want me to do or be this week?" and "How does God invite me to change?"

- Each person prays for the person on their right, at the end of the session, and throughout the week.[3]

Remember, however, that this study and sharing are not important just for those interested in attending the courses being offered. *Each* person is an important part of the Body of Christ, *every* person needs to be deepening their relationship and understanding of God. Lifelong Christian formation is therefore an important component to be integrated throughout a Spirit-filled community. But while those on fire with the Spirit will seek out specific programs and opportunities, the others may need a specific invitation to join in the instruction of the fundamentals and in Christian spirituality, until all are included.[4]

Fellowship

"Baptism is an initiation into the Christian community through being taught the Bible and being introduced to Christ," according to one of the congregations. And the Book of Common Prayer asks us, "Will you who witness these vows do all in your power to support these persons in their life in Christ?" (BCP, 303). Fellow Christians may share their stories, or, perhaps, they may set the environment or atmosphere that allows one to draw near to God. In one congregation church members and sponsors come to a session of their commitment program and give testimony about what their baptism and life in the Christian community has meant for them. Each person comes to a place in life where one can see and hear and then find God—and it is one's own encounter. But it needs to be interpreted in light of others' experiences as well as one's own. And so William Countryman, in writing about priesthood, acknowledges that "one person . . . may become more attentive than another and may therefore come to be recognized as someone who knows the secrets and who can minister out of them; but . . . the secrets are never *taught* . . . They are only experienced. But they require interpretation."[5]

Robert Banks states that for the early church, "According to Paul's understanding, participation in the community centered primarily around *fellowship*, expressed in word and deed of the members with God and one another. . . . The focal point of reference was neither a book nor a rite but *a set of relationships*, and that God communicated himself to them not primarily through the written word and tradition, or mystical experience and cultic activity, but *through one another*."[6] Therefore fellowship can be an ongoing tool that assists in finding the loving God, in interpreting all of life's experiences in terms of God, in supporting people during difficult times, in developing loving service, in challenging new personal and spiritual growth, and in pointing us back to God when we lose focus or get off track.[7]

Several congregations in this study reported just such a loving and supporting atmosphere. One said, "We are all family. We love to see each other on Sunday and throughout the week. No one is talking behind each other's back. Peace is passed to everyone. There is an acceptance of everyone."[8] Another congregation reported, "We try to welcome everyone no matter how they're dressed; try to help them out if we can. We have an awareness of each other. There is an informal process that if someone doesn't show up, we call them right after the service. If they need prayers, we contact the prayer chain." And still another reported: "We have a genuinely warm and familial congregation. You feel like you're home—almost like you can put your feet on the furniture. It's like, 'See how they love one another.' "

Being in loving relationships with others helps people to develop and mature, and brings out the best in them. This fullness of humanity in the Christian is the reflection of the image of God. How, though, can this be fostered in a congregation? Each community has been called by the Spirit, in their own way, to discover who they are. An example of this happened at a congregation where a rector of thirty-one years retired and the people took the time in an interim period to really investigate who they were and what they wanted. They formed teams and liked it. They decided that they wanted a priest who would support the team concept because they wanted it to continue. Additionally, Beth Ely suggests that churches find something, a local ministry, that everyone in the congregation can participate in, and feel valued doing, and then do it together in order to build fellowship as well as bridges within the community.[9]

Another fundamental way to *be* church rather than just *attend* church is through the formation of small groups. The use of smaller groupings was found to be quite valuable to several of the larger congregations studied, while many of the smaller congregations already functioned in that manner. An example of this is Holy Trinity in Vale, Oregon; as a family-size congregation it is a small group in itself. "It is a congregation where Vestry meetings and Parish meetings are all the same body."[10] But for one of the larger congregations "in order for us to grow both in depth and in numbers we need to respond to the deep need people have for connection, for real relationship and opportunities for faith sharing. This is best done when parishes provide small groups for nurture and support. These groups will continue to have a focus outside of themselves. They will exist for the greater vision of bringing people to know the love of God and to offer themselves for mission and ministry."

Many types of small groups that can promote Christian fellowship are possible. Such groups include support groups, study classes, Bible study and reflection, prayer and praise, fellowship, sports, dinner circles, leadership teams, staff meetings, vestry, committees or commissions, ministry teams, and missionary trip members. The groups can exist through the church, or in the neighborhoods, work settings, or elsewhere.[11]

Of the congregations studied, opportunities for small group activities were offered by 54.8 percent. Many congregations were already small and did not offer additional fellowship groups (38.7%). Just 6.5 percent of those congregations interviewed that were large enough to do so did not offer any type of small group.

Overall many of the small groups in existence were focused on Bible study, or prayer, or both (47.1%). Other groups included fellowship (23.5%) or support groups (11.8%). An additional 5.9 percent of the congregations offered several

Figure 10. Small Groups Offered?

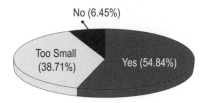

types of groups at the same time. One church in the northwest reports that their small group activity "is the healthiest thing we do. The groups include sharing, prayer, study, and care. Ours is a church *of* small groups. Affinity between members in a small group is what keeps them together, but it also can keep them from multiplying. Short term duration projects of six weeks helps [*sic*] to keep the groups open to growth and multiplication."

Figure 11. Types of Small Groups

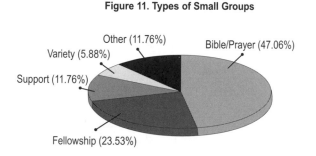

Fellowship at its best is a reflection of the triune nature of God. This relational reality is evident in the language used by the Christian faith: "Belonging to the body of Christ," "communion with Jesus and each other," "entering the kingdom of God," "reflecting the image of God to the world," and "Christian community."

> The communion with the HOLY and with one another that characterizes priestly ministry is not only a means to some further end, but a participation in the goal itself. To be intimately connected with one another, to serve as priests to one another, together in the gracious presence of TRUTH, of REALITY, of the HOLY, of GOD—this is not only the way we grow in apprehension of the arcane border country; it is already, in itself, a taste of human life as it was meant to be from the beginning.[12]

For one of the congregations that means: "We take the baptismal covenant in the prayer book very seriously. We are to bring people into the kingdom and help them to grow."

The Breaking of the Bread

Food is a basic element of life. Meals not only sustain the body, but the bonds formed in acquiring, preparing, and sharing the food also nourish these persons in their entirety. Through eating together families can become closer, friendships can become stronger, strangers can become allies, and enemies can celebrate a truce. It is therefore no surprise that a covenantal agreement uniting two parties is full of rich symbolism. The covenant is enacted (and later reenacted) through sacrificing a life, sharing this life together through a meal, and ultimately results in the creation of a new bond of existence. Sharing a covenantal meal is sharing life.

In the congregations studied many spontaneously mentioned the importance of being open and welcoming, respecting the dignity of any and all persons who chose to join the congregation for Eucharistic worship and for communal life. A few expressed the idea that the Episcopal way—or perhaps the way of their particular congregation—was not meant for everyone and that some specific people might be more comfortable elsewhere. Roy Oswald in *Making Your Church More Inviting: A Step-by-Step Guide for In-Church Training*, suggests, though, that even those congregations who think they are welcoming may not in fact give a cordial welcome to those who are dissimilar in appearance to their regular members. Take an objective look at the members in your congregation. Oswald maintains, "An ultimate goal of every parish should be to become so heterogeneous that it offers a genuine warm welcome to all shapes, sizes, races, and sexual orientations, regardless of their dress, history, or cleanliness. There is no question about God's love of them. Each is a unique child of God; there is a special ache in God's heart for each of them. Someday we may mature to the point where we are able to love them as God loves them. In the meantime we need to work at this, becoming more heterogeneous one step at a time."[13] Several congregations mentioned the importance of being an Episcopal presence for the local community. Indeed, it is good for each member to reflect the image and presence of God in the midst of the congregation, and for the congregation to stand reflecting the presence of God in the midst of its neighboring community. This, in fact, is an example of the priesthood of all believers: "You are a chosen race, a royal priesthood, a holy nation, God's own people, in order that you may proclaim the mighty acts of him who called you out of darkness into his marvelous light" (1 Peter 2:9). With openness, each person has the potential to be sacramental: to recognize and hold the door open to God's kingdom, to serve and share God's covenantal meal with others.[14]

The Prayers

Those baptized in the Episcopal Church today commit themselves to "the prayers"—the *official* prayers, which are the modern rituals of today's institutional church. These are contained in the Book of Common Prayer [E+], which is based on the *ancient* prayers of the apostles and the early followers of Jesus: the prayer Jesus taught his disciples; prayers prayed in Jesus' name; prayers that healed physically, mentally, and spiritually; praise; prophecy; psalms; and other *intimate* prayers inspired by the Holy Spirit [M+]. Biblical examples of these experiences of prayer in the early church include: "When they had prayed, the place in which they were gathered together was shaken; and they were all filled with the Holy Spirit and spoke the word of God with boldness" (Acts 4:31); "Pray in the Spirit at all times in every prayer and supplication. To that end keep alert and always persevere in supplication for all the saints" (Ephesians 6:18).

> Prayer is intimate conversation with God—real, demanding, loving, and engaged conversation between a real person and the real, living God. This conversation initiates, sustains, and augments a dynamic relationship full of risk and joy. We bring to this relationship the whole of who we are—history and culture, body and personality, affectivity and sensibilities, training and work. We bring to this relationship our very own memories, hopes, sorrows, disappointments, and achievements; we bring our very own deepest joys, most humiliating moments, and most excruciating pain. We bring our selves to the One who loves us most completely.[15]

Prayer, like talking about God in the church setting, is often assumed. If the assumption is right and if real prayerful people [M+] come together for the business of the Christian community [E+], great things can come about. "I tell you the truth, anyone who has faith in me will do what I have been doing. He will do even greater things than these" (John 14:12–14 NIV).

But often people are rushed and there seems to be much that needs to be accomplished for the ministry of Christ and for the individual church community. "In any event, do not give way to the temptation to skip over this time for personal spiritual growth [M] in order to 'get down to business' [E]. These times help people make the transition from their daily activities to the spiritual business of the session, and they pay rich dividends in the increased ability of participants to focus on the job at hand."[16] For if real ongoing spiritual lives are only represented by token "opening prayers," or if even the prayers are skipped over, so that the people can get down to business, then "You do not have in mind the things of God, but the things of men" (Mark 8:33b NIV) [E-]. The accomplishments of such a congregation may be successful by business standards, but not necessarily true to God's vision. "One of the bitterest choices the people of God have made is to try to figure out a way to have both, the kingdoms of this world and the kingdom of God. . . . One way is to live with the distortions the church has imposed. . . . We have been comfortable living with these distortions because they allowed us to feast at the tables of the empire six days a week and then bow down to archaic rituals the seventh day as a kind of death insurance, in case there really is a sweet by-and-by. Meanwhile, the institution got the money to build its church buildings and carry on its increasingly elaborate and irrelevant fantasies."[17]

In the congregations that were studied who used God language, very real, and at times intense, prayer was recounted. Opportunities for these experiences such as frequent prayer days and retreats, Bible study and prayer groups, spiritual direction, as well as earnest study and commitment to Christ were mentioned. Also included were the renewal of baptismal covenant, serious prayer and discernment as a basis of the staff/team meetings, and grappling with disagreements by studying the biblical models prayerfully. These people apparently do believe that they have experienced God's goodness, mercy, and love. Their energy comes from the Holy Spirit and it showed.[18]

Questions for Reflection

1. The Greek word *koinonia*, which is often translated as "fellowship," is perhaps better rendered as "partnership." What is the difference in your experience between fellowship and partnership?

2. What would *partnership* with God and the Christian community look like for you individually? For your church community?

3. How might *partnership* affect "continuing in the apostles' teaching, in the breaking of bread, and in the prayers" (Acts 2:42, BCP 304)?

CHAPTER 8

Return to the Lord

What would it look like . . .

> *if every Sunday Eucharist were a reminder to me of deeply meaningful experiences I'd had of God's love for me?*

> *if I had a deep sense of how my faith could be good news to others—and I had an immediate way to invite friends, neighbors, and co-workers to experience it for themselves?*

> *if I saw God's presence and the potential for sacramental moments in every arena of my life?*

> *if I had experienced the kind of spiritual discernment that encourages honest questions more than easy answers?*

> *if I took up the Great Commission to make disciples by inviting others to join a people who take seriously the Great Commandment to love as God loves us?*

> *if I were more deeply in touch with who I am in Christ?*

> *if a small group of people at my church really knew me, cared about me, and were there to support me in my life and walk with Christ?*

> *if I had a deep sense of God's call for me, and of the gifts God has given me to live into it?*

> *if I were discovering a life of prayer that energized and refreshed me?*

> *if I had a sense of walking in my twenty-first century life with saints through the ages?*

> *if my practice of faith came out of a sense of who I really am, and not*

just who I think I ought to be?

if I were excited about a path forward to keep growing as a Christian?[1]

> **Will you persevere in resisting evil, and,**
> **whenever you fall into sin,**
> **repent and return to the Lord?**
> (BCP, 304)

But when he came to himself he said . . . I will get up and go to my father, and I will say to him, "Father, I have sinned against heaven and before you . . ." But while he was still far off, his father saw him and was filled with compassion; he ran and put his arms around him and kissed him. (Luke 15:17–20)

The authors of the 1979 Book of Common Prayer understood that it was not a matter of *if* one would sin but rather *when*. "Human beings were not created good, perfect, programmed. Human beings were created *free*. Of all God's creations, human beings alone had the choice of whether to respond to God as God wanted them to, or to go another way. The Lover is always vulnerable to the beloved. The beloved may always say no."[2] And so the Episcopal prayer book responded to the need to strengthen the expressions of penitence in the baptismal rite by reminding Christians to be prepared to resist evil, and when priorities were turned away from God's love, to be willing to recognize it, repent, and return to the Lord of the covenant.[3]

Repentance, although it has negative connotations, is really a very positive action of *renewing one's covenant with God* who, in love, mercy, and generosity, is always ready to take one back [**M+**]. Being willing to own up and take responsibility for one's shortcomings and ask for forgiveness is a freeing step. Plus, sin and the need for God's help is one thing that all of humanity has in common. So dealing honestly with one's sins can actually open communication lines both with God and one's fellow human beings.[4]

Repentance is an ongoing task and commitment to put off the negative ways [**M- and E-**] and acquire positive [**M+ and E+**] habits. This requires daily, almost constant, effort at times. "Many of us *have* chosen a halfhearted way, and we're *not* always willing to do what God is calling us to do . . . We refuse to acknowledge, develop, and use our main talents, whatever they may be. We do not allow God to make contact with us and help us find out what God is calling us to do. Most of all, we fail to put ourselves at God's disposal as we go about our daily lives, whatever they may include."[5]

That is not the way you learned Christ!
For surely you have heard about him and were taught in him, as truth is in Jesus. You were taught to put away your former way of life, your old self, corrupt and deluded by its lusts, and to be renewed in the spirit of

your minds, and to clothe yourselves with the new self, created according to the likeness of God in true righteousness and holiness.
(Ephesians 4:21–24)

But because of the human tendency to sinfulness or selfishness, it's hard to know if one is really in tune with God. The answer is in simply trying; studying what Jesus calls us to, being open to the Holy Spirit's guidance, and trusting that God will help. This doesn't all just happen by thinking about it. Also, at times, one or another may be called away from the constant action of ministry and mission to prayerful reflection on the past, planning for the future, or other means necessary to prepare oneself for an even closer relationship to God.[6]

And the call to repentance is not just for individuals; Christian communities, too, can lose their identity of being a body of faith. As the church organization loses sight of its true purpose and moves into maintenance mode [**E-**] or when individuals or groups push for their own agendas [**M-**], the covenant with God is forgotten. This is especially problematic in churches, since those people who are seeking God are often looking to the churches to be a true community of faith. Churches "in name only . . . are not building up the Body of Christ and the kingdom of God, but tearing down and destroying lives."[7] So, in order to know how they stand before God, it seems appropriate that congregations and the corporate church consciously participate in a careful examination of conscience [**E+**].[8]

And it is through such an honest and overt self-accounting that the church will be able to change its longstanding failings, the bad habits that have become norms. But not much can be done as long as faults are ignored, taken for granted, or purposely hidden. For it is not until such sins are recognized, named, and owned that the work of repentance and forgiveness can begin.[9] Honesty with God, and oneself, and each other is the key to repentance and change. The work of repentance is hard, especially since God's ways call one away from the all-surrounding temptations and tendencies that may have become habits, cultural dictates, or ingrained mindsets. One simple example of this is the norm of being "nice." Christian harmony is instead accomplished by speaking honestly, but lovingly, and working with God's Holy Spirit to sort out individual differences of opinion. "The Spirit works toward reconciliation and harmony among people. . . . However, there is no easy rule. Sometimes the Spirit's prophetic work is divisive rather than unitive, at least for a time, as when it leads us to protest injustice. In addition, there are forms of superficial placidness that actually entail a 'tyranny of the majority,' violating true harmony."[10] Being "nice" in these cases could be considered a sinful avoidance of God's spirit of truth. The tendency for churches to focus mainly on survival and maintenance, or existing primarily for the benefit of its paid staff, is another example of a powerful temptation, because it is part of their nature as institutions.[11] Verna Dozier in *The Dream of God* comments that "the institutional church, from the resurrection community to the present day, has rejected [Jesus] since the day of his death in favor of something more reasonable, more controlled and more controllable, more human." And in so doing, she says, "Christianity has journeyed far from what Jesus of Nazareth was about."[12] Another example is that relying solely on "successful" business tactics (such as advertising, brand recognition, and appealing to the masses) to revive a dying church seems to be becoming a norm. But this will not work, since this approach is just attempting to improve one side of the polarity (moving from **E-** to **E+**). The problem is that in this effort the congregation avoids God's methods and therefore will remain simply a business enterprise. This method may appear to have some success but it will not really improve the whole system in the long run.[13] It's the covenantal promise of repentance (as well as polarity management) that reminds one that the only real answer is to move out from the negative place to the positive experience (from **E-** to **M+**), that is, returning to the Lord of the covenant and reentering the kingdom of God.[14] "His father saw him . . . he ran and put his arms around him and kissed him" (Luke 15:20).

The congregations that were studied were asked several questions that relate to the issues of repentance and of being prepared for the constant need to refocus: Do you have a method of conflict resolution in place? What issues, concerns, or obstacles do you face? What would you like to do next? What do you need to change? Regarding conflict resolution, the underlying assumption was that all congregations would have to deal with various conflicts on an ongoing basis as a part of human nature, since "differences of opinion and understanding will naturally arise even in the healthiest of settings."[15] Patricia Page, in *All God's People Are Ministers: Equipping Church Members for Ministry*, explains the problem, "The church's equipping of the saints for ministry must include training in negotiation and conflict management. Too often the church is the place where we deliberately avoid conflict. So strengthening for the ministry of reconciliation can begin in our own community."[16] Most of the congregations that were studied, however, had not developed a specific method. Fifteen percent reported using either a biblical model or praying together. One of them explained saying, "Some of the answers are spiritual" [**M+**]. A few had dealt with major conflicts and had utilized professional outside sources for mediation [**E+**].

Caroline Westerhoff, in *Calling: A Song for the Baptized*, observes that one's differences result in conflicts and confrontations that can have a creative force—a part of the dance, the rhythm of life: "The church is the place where we are equipped 'to carry on Christ's work of reconciliation in the world.' Part of this equipping must include our learning to confront each other so that we can confront the world with God's love. If we who claim to be created in the divine image and fed with the power of Christ's body and blood cannot entertain healthy conflict among ourselves, how can we expect to do so anywhere else?"[17]

In analyzing future directions and issues to be addressed, the goal listed most often was increasing the members' involvement, which was mentioned by 22.5 percent of the respondents. Two groups of 15 percent each were studying their identity and future direction due to either a change in clergy staff or a need to increase attendance. Increasing small groups, developing ministries, dealing with finances, increasing evangelism efforts, and developing more open attitudes in the congregation were each mentioned by 10 percent. Developing prayer, fellowship, youth programs, and a usable structure were each listed as goals by 5 percent. Education was also mentioned (3%).

Knowing where to go next is good. Being willing to start that journey is important. Looking forward to the covenant relationship is key.

> It's going to be a long process—realms you never dreamed existed. All of the human issues will come up and be dealt with. And you should be afraid of it. If you're not having a difficult time, you're not doing it right. Truly speak the truth in love to each other, both in conflict and struggle, and then in times of affirmation.[18]

Questions for Reflection

1. How do you currently handle conflict in your personal life? At church?

2. In the ancient world, when evil struck, the lord with whom one had an allegiance would come to the rescue if one would but call upon him. Even mentioning the name of one's powerful protector could get one's enemies, fearing retribution, to abate. Consider the following passage:

> Be strong in the Lord and in his mighty power. Put on the full armor of God so that you can take your stand against the devil's schemes. For our struggle is not against flesh and blood, but against the rulers, against the authorities, against the powers of this dark world and against the spiritual forces of evil in the heavenly realms. Therefore put on the full armor of God, so that when the day of evil comes, you may be able to stand your ground, and after you have done everything, to stand. Stand firm then, with the belt of truth buckled around your waist, with the breastplate of righteousness in place, and with your feet fitted with the readiness that comes from the gospel of peace. In addition to all this, take up the shield of faith, with which you can extinguish all the flaming arrows of the evil one. Take the helmet of salvation and the sword of the Spirit, which is the word of God. And pray in the Spirit on all occasions with all kinds of prayers and requests. With this in mind, be alert and always keep on praying for all the saints. (Ephesians 6:10–18 NIV)

Does this passage help you understand how God, as Lord, will assist you in resisting evil and deal with your transgressions? Why or why not?

CHAPTER 9

Will You Proclaim?

Many people are frightened at the thought of being expected to "evangelize." They don't think they have what it takes to talk to someone about Jesus. Priscilla King from Bellows Falls, Vermont, shows how proclaiming the good news can easily and simply flow from one's love for God and community through consciously choosing to share that love through everyday actions and kind words.

Immanuel: It means "God with us." Immanuel Episcopal Church: What a beautiful church! Yes, it certainly is that. It was built by loving hands; and, always cared for. Built to be God's house of worship, love, and fellowship. Built for God's disciples, apostles who were sent into the world on a mission to spread the word of God, Jesus Christ and the Holy Spirit.

We do this in many ways through our gifts of ministry. Our church ministries include: outreach programs; nurturing our children through our wonderful Sunday school; our faithful choir with beautiful musical teachings; our Holly Jolly program at Christmas to bring joy to children and adults; our Monday suppers to offer refreshment of body, mind and companionship. We offer our space to musical groups and programs, Falls Playschool, and we reach out ecumenically to other churches both local and statewide. We offer our church because it is God's, and we are accessible and accountable in His name. Our altar guild is another aspect of our ministry to Immanuel. It is not work or a chore. It is a time to handle holy things with reverence showing devotion and faithfulness through Christ our Lord.

Our other ministries, beyond the walls, are *countless*.

All of these are done by Christ's apostles. Now I say to you. What are your gifts, your ministries, which you can offer to God through your love? Ministry is the focus of who we are, nurtured by our life in Christ to do the work that was given us to do. We need you. You need us. You will be rewarded through your efforts of helping others of showing your love, wisdom and grace from God. All of us are apostles whether out in the world, in the church, or in our homes. All of us have gifts. How can we not offer ourselves, our gifts of thanksgiving and praise to God our Father, Jesus Christ, and the Holy Spirit!

As we ask in the prayer after communion, "Now send us forth to be your people in the world to proclaim God's good news in Christ Jesus."[1]

Will you proclaim
by word
and example
the Good News of God in Christ?
(BCP, 305)

Go and tell John what you hear and see. . . . (Matthew 11:4–6)
Then Jesus ordered them to tell no one; but the more he ordered them, the more zealously they proclaimed it. (Mark 7:36)
Whenever you enter a town . . . say to them, "The kingdom of God has come near to you." (Luke 10:8–9)
"He has been raised; he is not here. . . . But go, tell his disciples . . ." and they said nothing to anyone, for they were afraid. (Mark 16:6–8)
"As the Father has sent me, so I send you." When he had said this, he breathed on them and said to them, "Receive the Holy Spirit."
(John 20:21–22)

In the first century the term *gospel* was a technical term referring to "good news" that was meant to be heralded, meant to be proclaimed. Often this would be good news of success in battle.[2] And so, in this case, the battle has been waged against the types of evil, sin, and death that are realized in the doubt, betrayal, denial, abandonment, and execution of Jesus. The victor is the Lord of the covenant, who raised Jesus from the dead; who, instead of smiting the evildoers, forgave them. Yahweh invites all to accept citizenship into the kingdom and to live as heirs. All are invited to this joyous celebration of ultimate victory over the realm of evil and death. The worship guide of one of the interviewed congregations spelled it out like this: "Everyone is invited to receive Communion at God's Table. This is the family meal of all baptized Christians; all others who hunger for God are welcomed as honored guests." Thus all of creation can be seen as sacred again—as it was in the beginning—all that God creates is good. "Jesus . . . allowed his nearness with GOD to be manifest in his living of everyday life. . . . He reconnected the HOLY and the everyday . . . in a way that gave reverence to the PRESENCE that was already there."[3]

The topic of God is not something just for an intellectual or snazzy mono-logue in the Sunday sermon. In Michael Chase's congregation the people want someone to speak from their hearts and experience.[4] The good news is spread by those who believe, by those who have experienced God's power, those on God's side, those in a covenant relationship, those who can stand alongside God and are not swayed by the other side. Barbara Wendland, in *God's Partners: Lay Christians at Work*, reminds us that "sometimes you're a lens that someone else looks through to see God, whether or not you intend to be. Who you are and what you say and do can help clarify someone's picture of God."[5] This can be especially true if one thinks and lives everything in terms of one's Lord and his reign. Richard Broholm gives examples of how this can happen in "Toward Claiming and Identifying our Ministry in the Workplace": "The ministry of celebrating is that of recognizing and calling attention to the truth of God's presence, and the in-breaking of God's kingdom in our everyday affairs. This may include the celebrating of the newly identified and claimed gifts of our co-workers, recognizing and affirming moments of grace or the discovery of a new sense of God calling us, and remembering past events in which others experienced the liberating truth of God's love."[6] Practicing Christians constantly proclaim by their very lives the word and example of the good news of God in Christ. "The [baptismal] candidate promises to move among the people she or he encounters with intentionality, offering the ministry of presence, seeing herself as Christ's representative in all places."[7]

It is God alone who inspires people with the desire to bring people to Christ.[8] The result of one's belief and experience of God's good news of merciful love is to actually tell others about it so that they, too, can personally share in the awesome and intimate experience. "Every Christian who has a saving relationship with Jesus Christ should be ready to tell somebody what they have seen and heard through Christ. They should be ready to witness to someone else about God's amazing and saving grace. . . . In order to testify about what God has done in our lives we have to give honor and glory to God, and develop a close personal relationship with God."[9] As a Christian, one will want to introduce one's family, friends, coworkers, and everyone one meets to God.

> Spontaneous expansion begins with the individual effort of the individual Christian to assist his fellow, when common experience, common difficulties, common toil have first brought the two together. It is this equality and community of experience which makes the one deliver his message in terms which the other can understand, and makes the hearer approach the subject with sympathy and confidence. . . . The speaker . . . speaks from his heart because he is too eager to be able to refrain from speaking. His subject has gripped him. He speaks of what he knows, and knows by experience. The truth which he imparts is his own truth. He knows its force. He is speaking almost as much to relieve his own mind as to convert his hearer, and yet he is as eager to convert his hearer as to relieve his own mind; for his mind can only be relieved by sharing his new truth, and his truth is not shared until another has received it. This his hearer realizes. Inevitably he is moved by it. Before he has experienced the truth himself he has shared the speaker's experience.[10]

Jesus himself, as an itinerant preacher, practiced this type of sharing the good news of his Father's kingdom.

"The mission of each Christian is, then, to bring to every arena of daily life, in deed and word, the good news of God's work in Jesus Christ. These arenas include our daily work, our homes, our local communities, the wider world (of society, culture, economics, and government), our leisure time, and our faith community. In more traditional language, the mission is to proclaim and work, in deed and word, for the reign of God in all human life and the creation."[11] In doing this Christians add their own personal stories and testimonies of God's love to the church traditions, the Hebrew Scriptures, and the New Testament accounts. "Every baptized Christian is a storyteller by being a story-liver—one who lives the story—with a lifestyle outlined well in the baptismal covenant as found in the Episcopal Book of Common Prayer."[12] In sharing their stories, their lives, they make personal connections and build up a community of support and a deeper conviction to the truth.

> Upon the speaker, too, the effort to express his truth exercises a profound effect. The expression of his experience intensifies it; it renews it; it repeats it; it enlightens it. In speaking of it he goes through it again; in setting it before another he sets it before himself in a new light. He gets a deeper sense of its reality and power and meaning. In speaking of it he pledges himself to the conduct and life which it involves. He proclaims himself bound by it, and every time that his speech produces an effect upon another, that effect reacts upon himself, making his hold upon his truth surer and stronger.[13]

One's life, one's words, and one's actions themselves will be a witness to the Christian lifestyle—a witness to a life lived in the presence of God and of following the teachings of Jesus.

Presumably, the church organization [E+] is one of the primary means of introducing someone to God. For instance, Bible study groups can be a structured way to talk about one's experience with God. Mary Ann Hinsdale, in *It Comes from the People*, describes this type of group: "The makeup of the reflection groups consisted of members from different churches in the community, as well as those who did not profess allegiance to any church. Some of the participants described themselves as 'not regular churchgoers' but commented on the fellowship experience, saying that if church were more like what they had experienced in the Bible sessions, they might attend church."[14] But the organization is often concerned with increased membership in the organization, participation in Episcopal orientation programs, or the subsequent care in fitting the new members into the existing community's structure and dynamics [E], instead of on the budding relationship between the new Christian disciple and God [M+].[15] One interviewee reminds us that "since all Christians are evangelists and ministers, church members need to become involved in proclaiming their belief in God and sharing their spiritual experiences beyond their Sunday morning friends to the other people in their lives." The apostle Paul's mission assemblies were able to turn into viable independent Christian communities, mainly because Paul trusted both the Lord and the Holy Spirit to empower those newcomers to whom he had proclaimed the good news.[16]

"When people accept the momentum of their baptismal covenant and the essential community in which they are included and embraced, evangelism happens, as a way of living more than as a program for church growth; yet, oddly, growth is what happens as a result!"[17] Were the recommended congregations excited enough about what God was doing in their midst to have developed organized evangelistic efforts to spread the good news, introduce people to God, and thus recruit new followers of Christ? Only 11 percent of those interviewed indicated that this area was a priority. Altogether about half of the congregations (51%) did maintain such endeavors on an ongoing basis. Twenty-six percent evangelized to some limited degree. Twenty-three percent did not evangelize at all. Sometimes congregations get in the mindset that they have "enough" people. Harriette Burkhalter is aware that in developing ministry teams there is a constant need to bring other people on the team. "It is necessary to keep adding people, but there is a bit of a sense that 'we're it.' "[18] Whatever type of structure is chosen for inviting others to share in the good news, it can't be an exclusive or limiting type of organizational method. "Indeed, the body does not consist of one member but of many. If the foot would say, 'Because I am not a hand, I do not belong to the body,' that would not make it any less a part of the body" (1 Corinthians 12:14–15ff).

Questions for Reflection

1. What good news would you like to share or "herald"?

2. Who would you like to be able to share this good news with? What is the first thing you might say?

3. A common truism is "Actions speak louder than words." Do your actions speak loud enough to identify you (or your congregation) as a follower of Christ?

CHAPTER 10

Christ in All Persons

In the mid 1990s, the staff and vestry of our parish decided to publish a pictorial directory. As families, individuals, and couples were signing up to have their pictures taken it became known that it was the intention of a gay couple in the parish to have their picture taken together for inclusion in the parish pictorial directory. A very powerful and influential parishioner got wind of this fact and approached the vestry demanding that the vestry members and the rector intervene and keep this picture out of the directory. An enormous conflict among the vestry members ensued. With prayer, time, and the help of a psychologist trained in conflict resolution, the matter was resolved.

The directory was delayed for six months, but when it was published the gay couple's picture was included. The mission statement of this parish is that "We strive to seek and serve Christ in all persons." Using our Baptismal covenant as our guide, we worked through this conflict and today are a stronger, healthier parish family. Regardless of how one feels about the hot button issues facing our church and society today, our parish looks to our Baptismal promises to keep us focused on what is really important to the body of Christ.[1]

> **Will you seek and serve Christ in all persons,**
> **loving your neighbor as yourself?**
> (BCP, 305)

Seeking Christ in all persons is illustrative of the incarnation in action. "We attend to the activity of the divine in our midst. . . . We are aware of those around us, others who also are created in the image of God. . . . We are alert to the creation as a whole. . . . We approach the world and its creatures as subjects to be cherished."[2] One seeks to find both God's image and the basic common elements of humanity, and to realize that all share both of these characteristics with each other person— the most pure, good, holy of people, as well as the most fallen, desperate, pathetic, wretched souls. "If we imitate Jesus' priesthood, we shall find ourselves . . . entering the company of 'tax collectors and sinners,' conversing on an equal footing with the unclean, gratefully accepting hospitality in the houses of 'Samaritans' and 'lepers,' justifying lapses from the purity code, and saying, with the authority of our own experience, 'Your sins are forgiven.'"[3] As we learn in the gospels, Jesus associated with both ends of this spectrum and all in between, recognizing everyone as brothers and sisters and God's children.

Serving Christ in all people and loving your neighbor as yourself means treating each person with the respect one would show Christ and caring for each person with the same level of care you would bestow on yourself. Richard R. Broholm states, "Providing information, ideas, skills, or ways of viewing reality can be profoundly empowering for others—especially if this is done so as not to foster dependency and servitude but competence and potency."[4] Countryman expresses it: "Priestly ministry is not a gift from the strong to the weak, but rather a sharing between persons fundamentally equal. . . . We stand beside one another sharing what we have found in the border country. We understand that we cannot stand above anyone else in the presence of GOD, only alongside."[5] Thus this type of ministry is not pity or mere charity, nor sitting on committees talking about action: instead, it is being willing to work together, to share meals, to break bread, with all others. Ministry is not something one does either within the church or in the world, but it is *constant* loving service. "Your purpose is to stand with God and see the world's needs from God's viewpoint. You are to trust that your deeds of love, no matter how imperfectly they may be conceived and carried out, will express God's love for the world."[6] The Church of the Transfiguration in Dallas, Texas, has a mission statement of "Seeking Christ in All Persons + Serving Christ in All Persons." Ellen Dingwall reports that they do everything there with this mission statement in mind.[7] And so it is not so much something one does, but who one is. It is about, not doing *for* the needy, but cultivating real relationships; it is about loving and caring for one another as Christ loved us. Those to whom one would minister also have their own gifts of ministry and loving service to share. Countryman states: "My argument is that all human beings are priests, by virtue simply of our humanity."[8]

Seeking and serving Christ in all persons is the job of each and every baptized Christian. Zabriskie states it: "To 'have a vocation' is to be baptized. To 'go into the ministry' is to be baptized."[9] Each Christian is to experience himself or herself as loved by God; each is also to know that God loves each member of the rest of humanity. Oswald and Friedrich explain that "the church's task is to take people who come in looking to be served and turn them into servant people. . . . Changing someone from a self-centered, grasping individual into a grateful, joyful, giving person is no easy task."[10] But as Christians they, too, share in God's love for them. This loving service is ministry, a key element of the Christian message and mission. One hundred percent of the congregations studied reported performing some type of service work. But Christian service goes beyond church-sponsored activities. The parish description brochure for Immanuel in Bellows Falls, VT says it well:

> The people gathered at Immanuel believe strongly that each individual has been given unique and precious gifts by a loving God, and that each individual is called to use these gifts in daily life. We understand this to be a call to minister in Christ's name, and we understand that our Baptism, grafting us into Christ, is the primary event that empowers us to ministry. We see our ministry taking place in the world . . . in our homes and community, at our jobs, with our family, friends, neighbors, colleagues, and with strangers we meet every day—through the using of our gifts to the fullest. We recognize that we are called to be Christ's presence in the world, carrying out Christ's ministry of reconciliation and forgiveness.[11]

The Role of the Priest

Within the Christian community there are different types of people called to play very different roles within the church. There are those whose charismatic talents lie in the congregation's spiritual life [M+] as well as those whose administrative skills lean more to the church's business side [E+]. Those chosen, trained, ratified, and ordained as clergy by this institution live within the organizational reality [E]. They may have talents and spiritual gifts, however, primarily in one or the other of these poles. Often, though, expectations may be that clergy function as one, or the other, and often as both spiritual leader and the manager of the church's earthly concerns. What is important for rectors and others in leadership positions, then, is to recognize their own strengths and weaknesses and be willing and attuned to welcome and encourage the various gifts of other members so that a balance can be nurtured throughout the body.[12]

St. Stephen's Episcopal Church, a small community of 33 families, realized they had a problem when their previous rectors had total responsibility and control over everything. This ongoing situation, supported by their bylaws, resulted in both alienation of the members and burnout of the clergy. "As part of our reflection before entering another search we determined that we needed to flatten the hierarchy by re-writing the bylaws. The intent was to spread administrative responsibility for the parish to the members of vestry and where necessary to paid staff. The intent of the community was that the primary role of clergy is to proclaim the Gospel, and act as a catalyst in building up the Body of Christ."[13] This effort has proved itself: "The bills are paid, the lights are on and the flowers grow. . . . This small congregation has four licensed Preachers, four Lay Eucharistic Visitors, five Lay Readers conducting services such as Morning Prayer, one ordained Deacon, and two postulants for the Priesthood. There is an abundance of resources."[14] By taking the time and effort to study and rewrite their bylaws, St. Stephen's immersed both its members and the clergy in dialog regarding their gifts and roles in the Christian community.

The answers of the interviewees to the inquiry regarding the role of the priest in each of the studied congregations were quite varied. The actual responses included descriptions ranging from someone to take care of us, to a CEO, to a community organizer, to a ranch hand or a miracle worker. In order to analyze these responses, each congregation's descriptions were compared and matched with the various biblical descriptions of the gifts and roles described by the early church (1 Corinthians 12:8–10, 28–30; Ephesians 4:11–12; Romans 12:6–8). An additional category was added to include those who expected their priests to perform sacraments, lead services, and/or be an icon. (Please see "Role of Priest" figure 8 in chapter 5, which details the spiritual gifts and the responses of the various congregations.)

The single largest type of response was that of being an administrator with 58 percent. Second highest was performing the sacramental role with 48 percent. Compassionately supplying pastoral care was also valued and mentioned by 45 percent of the congregations. Building up the Body of Christ (33%) and equipping others for ministry (30%) were also listed. Teaching (20%), exhorting or preaching (20%), and contributing wisdom or vision setting (18%) were not mentioned as much.

The following chart illustrates the varying responses regarding the role of the priest in their congregation based on the role of who was interviewed. It is interesting to note that only the ordained listed faith or a spiritual aspect as the priest's role. Staff and other non-ordained persons tended to see the priest's role as a pastoral one, whereas the seminary-trained priests tended to view it more as a teaching role.

Figure 12. Role of Priest Based on Role of Interviewee

Priest's Role	Respondents			
	Staff	Canon 9 Clergy	Seminary Trained Priest	Lay Member
Administrative	70%	50%	88%	75%
Spiritual	0%	17%	25%	0%
Pastoral	70%	50%	25%	63%
Teacher	20%	0%	56%	38%
Sacramental	50%	100%	19%	63%
Total interviewed	10	6	16	8

In the eleven congregations that used locally trained, Canon 9 clergy, or a combination of Canon 9 and seminary-trained clergy, 100 percent of the respondents used the language of "sacrament" to describe the role of the priest in their congregation, compared to 28 percent of the other twenty-nine congregations. Analyzing by role of interviewee, overall 50 percent of staff and 63 percent of other non-ordained persons responded that the role of the priest was sacramental. The real distinction is that, again, 100 percent of Canon 9 clergy described their role as sacramental while only 3 of the 16 seminary-trained clergy interviewed (19%) did so.

This understanding of priest as sacramentalist has its roots or at least affirmation in the interpretation or practice of the older Title III, Canon 9. The canon itself simply referred to congregations "which cannot be provided sufficiently with the sacraments and pastoral ministrations of the Church through Clergy ordained under the provisions of Canon III.7."[15] The expectation of the canon's authors was that typical clergy offer both sacraments and pastoral ministry. The experience of Canon 9 congregations was that the ordained priest does not have to do everything and, in their situation, finding a part-time person who could attempt to do so was unlikely. So in these congregations those gifted for the more pastoral (rather than ritual) ministries were not typically ordained as priests; instead they may have been ordained as deacons, part of a "ministry team," or simply parishioners carrying out their gifts.

There also were fewer additional gifts or roles listed by the Canon 9 congregations to describe their priests: an average of 1.6 gifts compared to an average of 3 listed by the other congregations. The reason for this may be either that there are not as many activities in these small congregations requiring the priest's involvement, or that their other members' gifts have been recognized and affirmed by these congregations to perform these roles. Some congregations have come to do quite well without paid clergy, and feel comfortable with this model.[16] One congregation reported that they are at a point where it would be an alien concept to ask permission from a rector; it would be a tough thing for them to do. A priest in the role of "area missioner" expressed concern that some clergy will feel threatened with increased lay involvement, and the perception that their roles are being overtaken. But he feels that with the priest acting as missioner and the empowerment of lay persons, the clergy person is allowed to do what they really are called to be as priest, and that the others can do everything that they're called to be as well. He suggests asking, "What is God or the Holy Spirit really calling you to do?"

Eddy Hall and Gary Morsch, in *The Lay Ministry Revolution: How You Can Join*, remind us, "It is important for each of us to discover the ministries God is calling us to. If we try to do a little of everything, we will end up doing nothing well. Just as each part of the human body has certain functions, so God has given each member of the body of Christ specific jobs to do. The only way the body can work as God intends is for each member to do his or her own jobs well."[17]

Vocation and Discernment

We are offering three retreats this year where participants will have the opportunity to explore their spiritual gifts. We believe that ministry is the place where our great passion and the world's great needs meet. We want parishioners to minister where their gifts lie, rather than where the church needs work done. We believe that God will provide gifted people to carry out the mission of the church, and we want to help people find the ministry that God has for them. Our weekends are designed to help us:

- identify our special talents
- work with each other in small groups to identify gifts and consider the risks in actualizing them
- identify how our gifts may be used in ministry in response to God's love
- listen to God's voice through Bible study, journal and reflection time
- create communities to continue gift discernment.

Part of our mission statement says that we are called to "nurture each person's spiritual growth and ministry . . . invest our gifts as fully in the world as we do among ourselves." These workshops can prepare us to do so, as well as to become more fully the person that God has created us to be.[18]

"Wait for the gift my Father promised, which you have heard me speak about. For John baptized with water, but in a few days you will be baptized with the Holy Spirit" (Acts 1:4b–5 NIV). The Holy Spirit "leads us into all truth and enables us to grow in the likeness of Christ" (BCP, 852).[19] The Holy Spirit can help to discern or clarify one's vocation and empower one for living a life in covenant with God. The vocation is one of being called to come, follow Jesus; this vocation is one of being a reflection of God's image. A vocation is not so much what one does for a living, but a calling and response. Vocation is a covenant relationship of loving service to God enacted by one through *everyone* encountered and in *everything* in creation *throughout* life. David Lovelace reports that at St. John the Baptist, York, PA, "Gifts are shared through daily professional lives that impact the larger community. The parish serves to encourage and support many volunteer efforts in the community. It is difficult to think of an agency, service organization, volunteer group that does not include some member or influence from the parish."[20] Inside of this context of ongoing loving service, then, one naturally makes use of one's inborn talents, passions, and training, and is further strengthened by additional gifts that the Holy Spirit grants for particular tasks or occasions [M+].[21] Some people may easily discern their calling to loving service; for others it is realized in the doing or as the community affirms their actions.[22] In addition to private or individual prayer in listening for God's direction, the church organization can provide a systematic "discernment process" [E+] to help Christians become aware of the Holy Spirit's presence as well as their own spiritual gifts.[23]

A resource for *congregational* discernment is Oswald and Friedrich's book *Discerning Your Congregation's Future: A Strategic and Spiritual Approach*. This book describes a discernment process for the congregation as an entity in itself incorporating strategic planning methods with a focus on God, prayer, and various discernment tools. This work also includes Bernie Zerkel's "five principles that outline the connections between God, prayer, and the corporate discernment process."[24]

Several of the interviewed congregations (52%) reported having discernment methods by which their individual members could determine the gifts that the Holy Spirit was giving to each of them. A little more than half of these congregations were Canon 9 congregations. In the Canon 9 congregations the process was often used for non-ordained people to discern gifts that they would use as ordained Canon 9 clergy, or as part of a leadership ministry team to take the place of a clergy minister. Larger congregations expressed finding "lay leaders," people to be "raised up" from their general membership, but not necessarily ordained. Therefore, with this emphasis on finding organizational leaders and administrators (i.e., chairpersons), there was not an overall acknowledgment that *all* of the members in the congregations had viable gifts that needed to be recognized and accepted as important aspects of the body of Christ. But "in 1 Corinthians 12, Paul keeps the proper priority on the giver and coordinator of gifts. That sense of priority provides, as Paul suggests, an equality of gifts, because these sometimes strange and diverse gifts really work only as they are bound or 'glued' together by the Spirit."[25]

Several congregations who had completed a process of discernment in the past mentioned the need to do another one, indicating that the tools used for discernment were not necessarily incorporated into an ongoing process. In the larger congregations (whether there was a discernment process, or people were volunteers, or were volunteered by a staff member or clergy), getting the volunteers connected with the necessary resources, as well as starting up their ministry, was often mentioned as problematic. In addition to these initial contacts, long after someone's communal role had been discerned, maintaining ongoing support and giving and taking responsibility were also reported as continuing issues. Thus discernment for individuals can't be an isolated element, but developing service ministries needs to be integrated thoroughly in the congregation's life through support, fellowship, and perhaps mentoring as well.

Some of the recommended congregations, however, noted that the discernment process itself was an ongoing one. There may be a temptation, after some initial success in producing new persons and new energy, to shift the focus to the resulting new ministries. It is important to remember that discernment—learning to interpret and connect with God's Spirit—is an ongoing, developing relationship. Discernment should not be thought of as, nor limited to, merely a program or process. Victor Horvath maintains, "Once we end the covenant group, we can't end, the education needs to continue so that the next level, the next discernment process and the next covenant group starts. We need to continually name gifts and be open to the Spirit and how we work together. . . ."[26] For another congregation the initial process happened nine years ago, but it fell off. Now there is burnout and a need for them to be more intentional about starting it again. Jim Scheible described Total Ministry for his congregation as an ongoing process of training and growth, "One needs to think long term because formal additions to the team (especially priests) take a long time. People burn out and others move, so there is a need to plan ahead."[27] The solution is to build a continual and integrated discernment process of ongoing individual and group prayer, real communities of Christian support, and continuing education and adult Christian formation.

The congregations studied displayed a vast range in their efforts regarding the discernment of God's calling and members' responses with the resulting spiritual gifts. Overall, however, several specific concerns surfaced.

1. There was sometimes a focus on the gifts, and on the self, that is, the person and his/her talents instead of on God who is the giver of the gifts. This can come across as selfishness, self-centeredness, or possessiveness when using the gifts. In determining a person's role in the Body of Christ, a greater responsibility is involved beyond focusing merely on psychological tools, personality traits, or inborn talents and passions. "Sometimes spiritual gifts and talents are confused. While both are gifts from God and often work hand in hand, God has given all people talents. Spiritual gifts operate . . . in whom God's Spirit lives. . . . A spiritual gift is an ability to allow God's Spirit to touch the spirit of another person through you in a particular way."[28] Christians are "responsible," their motivation is a "response" to God; it involves their whole being, not just the things they do. God often calls people to grow and mature, to respond past their obvious talents or beyond ordinary expectations. In a trusting relationship the individual can let go of the limits placed on oneself (by self or by others) and develop beyond expectations. "Very truly, I tell you, the one who believes in me will also do the works that I do and, in fact, will do greater works than these, because I am going to the Father" (John 14:12). Humans are made in God's image, and as such each has a role of his or her own to play in the Body of Christ: "As one grows in love of God and an experience of oneness with God, paradoxically one grows also toward being more distinctively oneself."[29]

2. *Ministry* often brings to mind church work and especially ordained or clergy status in the church institution. But ministry (and Jesus often reminded his disciples of this) is actually based in loving "service."[30] It is hard to overcome the accepted mindset, though, because its influences come from more than one source. Sometimes a discernment team is created in a congregation to decide prayerfully which people will serve the church community in various capacities. Requesting the assistance of the Holy Spirit is an excellent approach; however, often the roles that are being considered are simply the typical functions a church needs in order to be accepted as a traditional Episcopal congregation, or to replace seminary-trained priests where they can no longer be afforded. Patricia Page refers to this type of approach as a *Slot Model*: "In such congregations mission is defined by what

has always been done and what has always been assumed to be God's will. The various jobs in the church are defined in terms of this stated mission (Sunday school teachers, church council members, maintenance persons, etc.), and then 'warm bodies' are sought to fill these slots."[31] When a congregation falls into this habit, it fails to open itself and its members to the full possibilities to which God is calling them. Yes, God may be pleased with attempts to be a full-functioning Episcopal Church, but the Holy Spirit always calls us beyond the present reality to accept more deeply Jesus' challenge to true authenticity. Moving beyond the familiar and the comfortable toward greater union with God and toward full Christian ministry may feel threatening and dangerous—but it's supposed to! Baptism is all about death to one's former existence and then new life in the service of the Lord.[32]

3. What percentage of people who are involved constitutes a successful number? "There's an old adage that in volunteer organizations: 'Ten percent of the people do ninety percent of the work.' What is your response to that?"[33] Nels Moller expressed concern that only 50 percent of the members of his congregation were well aware of the priesthood of the laity and have the knowledge that they need to do ministry, while the others don't feel called.[34] For him 50 percent is not enough, and in the smallest congregations even 100 percent participation does not provide the critical mass for what people often assume is necessary to be a adequately functioning church. *Each* person is important and indispensable. "In the New Testament dispensation of the Spirit (just as the priesthood) has been given to the whole people of God, not to select individuals."[35] There did not appear to be many congregations that intended, or that had a plan, to incorporate every single member in a fully functioning capacity. Some purposely indicated that they did not wish to appear "pushy," some were more willing to encourage a financial pledge than a personal commitment to involvement in some type of Christian ministry. Each person is given talents. "For it is as if a man, going on a journey, summoned his slaves and entrusted his property to them" (Matthew 25:14). Each will be held accountable. "After a long time the master of those slaves came and settled accounts with them" (Matthew 25:19). It is the responsibility of the Christian community to make its members aware of God's expectations through renewal and reaffirmation of the baptismal covenant. "As for this worthless slave [who buried his talent], throw him into the outer darkness, where there will be weeping and gnashing of teeth" (Matthew 25:30).

4. Finally, regarding the interview questions about "Discernment of gifts and empowerment of each member: How do people in your congregation discover/discern their spiritual gifts and ministries? How do they get involved?" Often the answers would be about identifying the various ministry *leaders* and how they would be supported in their new roles. In smaller congregations there was a tendency to describe how a team of both locally ordained and non-ordained ministers were identified to take over the role of the priest, or even, simply, how the discernment process for their Canon 9 clergy took place. The focus of the question was meant to be on involvement and incorporation of *all* the members, but there

seemed to be an underlying assumption by many congregations that the *real* ministry was performed by someone seminary-trained and ordained, and that the other styles of ministry were still something less. However, a few of the congregations *did* express difficulty and reluctance in using the typical terminology of "laity" to describe a Christian churchgoer. One of the interviewees commented that it is hard to use the term "lay" because we're all doing it together now. She told me that she wears the collar as a uniform much like a nurse wears white when working; the clothes symbolize the role she is performing for the people. Robert Tate commented, "We have found the words lay and volunteer to be problematic. We are striving to use the terms baptized and minister instead."[36]

Each baptized minister will need to engage in some type of "discernment process" in order to come to an awareness of God's action and prompting in his or her life. Congregations as a whole, too, need to make this a conscious effort. "The practice of discernment makes intentional a process of reflection on and participation with God's Spirit as the fundamental context in which we live and make choices. It is embedded in a variety of forms, all of which aim to check deception and nurture openness to the New Creation. The methods are easy. The practice, however, is challenging, painful, and complex."[37] There is no one formula for leading a congregation in a spiritual discernment process, but the key is prayer—both talking with God and believing that the Spirit will provide guidance.[38] Some people, either by nature or through practice have come to be able to communicate quite readily and freely with God. However, "mystical experiences [M+] are certainly not the only way we will come to know God because God will speak to us through Scripture, tradition, community, relationships, and events and experiences [E+]. What is needed in all cases is the gift of discernment so we are able to distinguish between messages from God [M+] and messages that stem from our own willfulness, our ego, or even our shadow" [M-].[39] Many people feel that they aren't able to figure out, for sure, what God's will for them may be. They perhaps don't really believe that the Holy Spirit will provide direction. Or perhaps they are afraid that they won't like what God has in store for them. Even after belief and trust in the goodness of God are grasped, hesitancy is common because people want to know what will happen, and they want to be in control [E-], but "all those things will sort themselves out under the guidance of the Holy Spirit [M+]. What is important now is that we begin."[40]

"He will baptize you with the Holy Spirit and fire."
(Matthew 3:11c)

Questions for Reflection

1. The Greek word *charisma* was used to describe the "bonuses" given on festive holidays to soldiers to honor and acknowledge the emperor or ruler. Christians' spiritual gifts can be referred to as "charismatic gifts." What gifts have you been given by God that go beyond your mere talents and skills? That is, can you identify gifts that go beyond your own abilities and can be acknowledged as unearned and coming straight from God's Spirit? How can you more often use these spiritual gifts to seek and serve Christ in all persons?

2. Although charismatic gifts are usually thought of in terms of individuals, can you identify such gifts that your congregation may have as a body?

CHAPTER 11

Every Human Being

Every three years representatives of each of the Episcopal dioceses from across the United States come together to discern and determine the future direction of the church organization. Over the years the Episcopal Church has made many resolutions concerning justice, peace, and the dignity inherent in God's creation. It has resolved:

- to established a ministry of community investment and economic justice through community development programs[1]
- to provide their own employees a living wage with health benefits and to model ethical labor practices, as well as to call upon the U.S. government to establish a living wage as the standard compensation for all workers[2]
- to promote nonviolence, valuing love, compassion, and justice, while rejecting violence as a means of solving problems[3]
- to acknowledge that homosexual persons are children of God[4]
- to begin discussion and action on principles of justice and accountability in the church workplace, recognizing that such issues should not be addressed apart from the Baptismal Covenant[5]
- to become a church committed to ending all forms of racism, acknowledging that their own ongoing acts of commission and omission have perpetuated racism in both church and society[6]
- to fund international nutritional, education, health care, and development programs in order to recognize the dignity of all human beings.[7]

> **Will you strive for justice and peace among all people, and respect the dignity of every human being?**
> (BCP, 305)

And what does the LORD *require of you*
but to do justice, and to love kindness,
and to walk humbly with your God? (Micah 6:8)

We are all God's children. "Have we not all one father? Has not one God created us? Why then are we faithless to one another, profaning the covenant of our ancestors?" (Malachi 2:10). Not just those who profess to be Christians, but all humans.[8] All are made in God's image. "So God created humankind in his image, in the image of God he created them; male and female he created them" (Genesis 1:27). Jesus continues with this conviction when he speaks of Yahweh as his father and by referring to his followers as his brothers and sisters: "Here are my mother and my brothers! For whoever does the will of my Father in heaven is my brother and sister and mother" (Matthew 12:49b–50). This common blood, this basic fact of our oneness in our human essence, is the basis for recognizing and respecting the dignity inherent in all human creatures and must be accepted at the core of one's being. For Paul, the incarnational reality and unity in Christ was what put people on an equal footing. No matter one's gender or rank, each person was empowered by the Holy Spirit for loving service for Christ. "Social privileges, no longer a mark of *distinction between* members of the community, could become an occasion for *service to* them."[9] Or the realization that "the more I experienced God's love, the clearer it became that I was . . . treating [people] as objects . . . not as hurting people who needed to be loved."[10] From this perspective it becomes easier to be "delivered from hardness of heart" (BCP, 391). "Love your enemies and pray for those who persecute you, so that you may be children of your Father in heaven . . ." (Matthew 5:44–45).

"Love implies reverence for one another. In every person, ourselves included, we see one whom GOD has created, chosen, loved, forgiven, welcomed, and celebrated. We therefore see each person as a complex and beautiful mystery, worthy of all this outpouring of GOD's gifts. . . . The beauty of this mystery, unique in each person, draws us to one another. It inspires our love, and our love allows us, even if just briefly, to transcend the distance between us."[11] As soon as this fundamental dignity is recognized and embraced, actions striving toward God's ultimate justice and peace become a natural corollary of one's covenant with God.

Very few of the congregations contacted for this study had overt social justice involvement as a priority. Hinsdale, in *It Comes from the People*, has noted that often there is not a correlation between the church organizations and community organizing efforts. Her observations include: "Faith and religious convictions [are] concepts that are often suspect in community organizing circles, since they are seen as dulling and prohibitive to the development process. . . . None of the church persons working with Ivanhoe actually lived in the community. . . . More problematic, however, was the 'task-oriented' attitude of some ministers, who saw themselves as only doing a specific 'job'"[12]; and she quotes Maxine Waller in saying, "The biggest obstacle I have in the community is churches. . . . the one group of people that has really stood in the way has been ministers. And the reason is because they're afraid they'll lose their little flock."[13] Just 19 percent of the congregations studied mentioned engaging in social justice activities, another 22 percent allowed for indirect activities, 31 percent admitted to handling such issues very cautiously, while 28 percent did not engage at all in that area. Those congregations who did indicate that they were involved generally listed several in-depth social service, mission work, or political involvement activities by those interested, rather than a parish-wide educational program or some other effort to move toward total participation. And yet, in addition to the baptismal covenant mandate of justice, peace, and dignity for all, resolutions passed at each Episcopal General Convention for at least the past fifteen years have called for awareness, training, involvement, and funding at every level and in every area of the church. Specific areas have included: economic justice, anti-racism, global peace and justice, environmental stewardship, justice and accountability in the church workplace itself, personal dignity, promoting a culture of non-violence, and urban justice and mission.[14]

Some of the questions that were asked of the congregations for this study regarded conflict resolution methods, service to all God's people, and participation in social justice issues, but the heart of this covenantal question is really much deeper. Dealing with the issues of dignity, justice, and peace often involves changing or addressing and confronting the very attitudes and underlying beliefs imbedded into societies and cultures. Thus this particular covenantal promise is consigned best, not just with an individual Christian's commitment and effort where they live and work, but on an organizational, church-wide scale as well.[15] "The object of social justice is improved institutions, not better individuals."[16]

Robert Greenleaf has studied personal and institutional responsibility in his *Servant Leadership: A Journey into the Nature of Legitimate Power and Greatness.* He challenges both his readers and their organizations to further growth by asking:

> Can you make of yours an institution in which the conditions of life in that institution raise *all of those* involved in it to a higher achievement as fulfilled persons than if they did their own things without the benefit of those conditions? Can you devise a disciplined participation that raises people's sights to nobler purposes than they would embrace if they were not constrained by that discipline? . . . Can you make of discipline the means whereby longer achievement *for the person—for every involved person*—is assured?"[17]

The Episcopal Church covenants with God to create or strengthen a Christian community that realizes and enacts a respect for the dignity of every human being. This will ground each community as well as the denomination to enter into God's justice and peace at every level.[18]

Questions for Reflection

1. What resolutions will *you* as an individual make before God as an indication that you are striving for God's justice and peace?

2. How does your congregation respect the dignity of every human being? List specific actions. How could this be done better? Give concrete examples.

CHAPTER 12

God's Help

Faithworks: Community, Worship & Action

To some that means the building itself, erected after decades of frustrated effort by a small African-American congregation.

To some it means the strange way donated materials, furnishings, expertise and labor all seemed to arrive right on cue.

To others it means the way a dozen congregations, never united before, crossed racial and economic boundaries to work together.

To everyone, the hands-on labor of building St. Philip's Episcopal Church in Greenville, S.C., for and with its parishioners has meant new friendships and enriched lives.

"It was God's timing," says parishioner Ann Marie Jones, one year after the church's dedication. "We'd been trying to build for years and years. . . . saving for years and years."

The 31-family congregation now gathers every week in a brand-new, carpenter gothic church. Painted in striking shades of mauve and merlot, the sanctuary feels surprisingly intimate, its soft color punctuated by dark-stained rafters that soar 42 feet above the pale, red oak floor.

For many it's a dream long deferred.

A modest mission

First established in 1914 as a mission church, St. Philip's was one of seven congregations founded for African-Americans in the Diocese of Upper South Carolina. For the last four decades, parishioners have met in a one-story, brick clad, cinder block building on the outskirts of Greenville. The modest structure served as both sanctuary and function hall and looked more like a warehouse than a place of worship.

The congregation dreamed of building "a real church." Raising money didn't come easily. Each generation tried, but there never seemed to be enough. Then two events coincided to change St. Philip's future forever: The bishop hired a new vicar, and the diocese formed the Reedy River Convocation.

The vicar, Beth Ely, believed communities should help build churches. Feisty and determined, she envisioned hands-on volunteers creating something beautiful just like in earlier days of barn-raisings. She wasn't quiet about her idea of a Habitat-for-Humanity-model church.

So, when the diocese formed new convocations and the 12 churches of Reedy River started casting about for projects, Ely's idea was a natural. Church leaders wanted something to work on jointly that would draw the congregations into closer relationship. The idea of a "church-raising" won enthusiastic endorsement.

Construction began on the $355,000 church in July 2002 after months of preparation, grant-seeking and fund raising. Volunteers arrived at the site to pound nails, pour concrete, paint, polish and place tiles. They came from every church in the convocation and some outside it.

They helped find furnishings and expert help. Sometimes the finds themselves seemed miraculous. . . .

Word spread like wildfire

As the building progressed and word of the "miracle church" spread, even non-Episcopalians started sending money, says Duncan Ely, Beth's husband. "Donations came from former vicars, from neighbors, even from a man in prison nobody knew."

Organizing "a collection of Episcopalians who'd never met each other" was a miracle in itself, he says.

"Every church in the diocese came together with us and worked in order that we have this," boasts parishioner Donice "Betty" Martin, exaggerating a bit. "Yes, it's a miracle. You see miracles every day just walking around."

'So many boundaries'

"We crossed so many boundaries," says Beth Ely, naming race, class, income. "But also age," she says. "Our elderly parishioners painted just like the kids did. We had people who were quite wealthy and people who really live on a fixed income working side by side. . . . We got comfortable with each other in a way that nothing else—no artificial forum, well-intentioned as they are—could have accomplished."

Ely calls the experience the most rewarding in her 15 years of ministry. Her parishioners and the other volunteers seem to feel the same.

"This is the best thing I have ever done in my life," says Margaret Brockman of Christ Church, Greenville. "I have done God's work." Parishioner Annette Smith has, too. "This building means so much to me. . . . I'd do anything for this church. If you see me in church, I be crying all the time because I am so rejoiced."

Architect [Dan] Beaman shares that emotion. "Not to sound corny or anything, but this was one of those times when the Holy Spirit was so evident, you knew you better get on board or get out of the way."

Says parishioner Martha Anne Mial, "I never thought I'd see this day . . . the new church, and my hands helped to place the stones."

A time to celebrate

The evening of the dedication, Jan. 30, 2003, hundreds of well-wishers and former volunteers came to celebrate with parishioners of St. Philip's. The bishop, the former bishop, the archdeacons and the mayor of Greenville (an Episcopalian) processed around the outside of the church to the light of Tiki torches and luminaria.

The thurifer swung a censor filled with aromatic herbs, invoking the Holy Spirit as the congregation sang a joyful Zulu song. Then, aided by ringing bells and clashing cymbals, drums, kazoos and maracas, the congregation entered for the Eucharist singing As the Saints Go Marching In.

"I was crying, crying . . . it was like we couldn't believe we had actually done it," says Phyllis Webb of the Church of the Redeemer, the coordinator of volunteers.

Former Bishop William A. Beckham, who when archdeacon had saved the perpetually struggling church from being closed, preached at the dedication.

"He was in tears," says Beth Ely. "We all were."

"It was just a tremendous challenge," says parishioner Janice Smith, "and we conquered it . . . through faith in God."

She looks around the old church hall where she grew up attending services, Sunday school, parish suppers.

A wide open, brightly painted corridor now links it to the new sanctuary. "This is family. This is home. This is love. Being with them has strengthened my faith."

"You know," says Beth Ely, "it's like the kingdom at work."[1]

(Written by Nan Cobbey, *Episcopal Life*)

I will, with God's help.

(BCP 304–5)

Jesus said to them, "Very truly, I tell you, the Son can do nothing on his own, but only what he sees the Father doing; for whatever the Father does, the Son does likewise. The Father loves the Son and shows him all that he himself is doing. . . . . I can do nothing on my own." (John 5:19–20, 30)

One person alone can do nothing of ultimate importance, but today's culture values independence, autonomy, and personal authority as signs of maturity—of making it on one's own.[2] God values each person's freedom to choose his or her own path and own allegiances. God is neither a controller nor a passive onlooker. God continually invites one to come home. "God will keep coming back to remind us of whose we are and who we are created to be."[3] "The meeting of Christians with their God is . . . analogous to the encounter between *adult* children and their father, where they are able to relate to him not only in the most intimate, but increasingly in the most mature, fashion."[4] And eventually one can mature enough to realize that there is an awesome responsibility in choosing to follow Jesus' way. "To be aware of grace, to personally experience its constant presence, to know one's nearness to God, is to know and continually experience an inner tranquility and peace that few possess. On the other hand, this knowledge and awareness brings with it an enormous responsibility. For to experience one's closeness to God is also to experience the obligation to be God, to be the agent of His power and love."[5] The Holy Spirit, however, in fact the whole of God, is there waiting to help—to be of loving service to *us*.[6] "We are not alone. . . . We need never rely on our own strength and courage, our own wisdom and behavior alone. We need not act as if the primary aim for our lives is to be effective or to make a difference, even if this is the message of our culture. Instead, we are to be concerned about faithful living and doing God's will, even when it appears futile. Further, to rely on God's grace and love is to acknowledge that God gives us what we need, not what we deserve, and we are to do likewise for each other."[7] Paradoxically, in no longer needing to be in control, one is now freer—freer to listen to, and talk with, and discover God—freer to accept God's new assignments and adventures.[8] In fact, the baptismal covenant makes one a partner in loving service with God. "You are a real partner whom God invites to share the responsibility for carrying out God's plan for the world. . . . No matter how unbelievable it may seem, or how overwhelmed you may feel, God keeps inviting you to partnership. This is God's answer to your deepest longings."[9]

"Praise God who made heaven and earth, who keeps his promise for ever. Do you believe and trust in God the Father, who made the world? *I believe and trust in him.*"[10] Fifty percent of those interviewed expressed themselves in terms that reflected belief and trust in God and a willingness to accept God's assistance—elements of a relational covenant with God. The forms these expressions took included relationship with God and/or Jesus, the importance of prayer, both individual and corporate; the activity, guidance, gifts, and expectancy of the Holy Spirit; discernment, trust, and acceptance of God's presence and will; God's revelation through Scripture; and the transformation in human lives that results from an ongoing experience of God's goodness and love.

Questions for Reflection

God asks, "Are you ready, then?"

1. What is your response?
2. What is the first thing you know you must do (with God's help)?

(Answer each question first as an individual, then as a congregation.)

Section Three

Prophecies, Dreams, and Visions

The Dream

And it shall come to pass afterward,
that I will pour out my spirit on all flesh;
Your sons and your daughters shall prophesy,
your old men shall dream dreams,
and your young men shall see visions.
Even upon the menservants and maidservants
in those days, I will pour out my spirit.

Joel

. . . .

Let us dream of a church

in which all members know surely and simply God's great love,
and each is certain that in the divine heart we are all known by name.

In which Jesus is very Word, our window into the Father's heart;
the sign of God's hope and his design for all humankind.

In which the Spirit is not a party symbol,
but wind and fire in everyone;
gracing the church with a kaleidoscope of gifts and constant renewal for all.

A church in which

worship is lively and fun as well as reverent and holy;
and we might be moved to dance and laugh;
to be solemn, cry or beat the breast.

People know how to pray and enjoy it—frequently and regularly,
privately and corporately, in silence and in word and song.

The eucharist is the center of life
  and servanthood the center of mission:
the servant Lord truly known in the breaking of the bread.
With service flowing from worship, and everyone understanding
  why worship is called a service.

Let us dream of a church

in which the sacraments, free from captivity by a professional elite,
are available in every congregation regardless of size, culture, location or
  budget.

In which every congregation is free to call forth from its midst priests and
deacons,
  sure in the knowledge that training and support services are available
  to back them up.

In which the Word is sacrament too, as dynamically present as bread and
wine;

members, not dependent on professionals, know what's what and who's who
  in the Bible,

and all sheep share in the shepherding.

In which discipline is a means, not to self-justification,
  but to discipleship
and law is known to be a good servant but a very poor master.

A church

affirming life over death as much as life after death,

unafraid of change, able to recognize God's hand in the revolutions,

affirming the beauty of diversity,
abhorring the imprisonment of uniformity,

as concerned about love in all relationships as it is about chastity,
and affirming the personal in all expressions of sexuality;

denying the separation between secular and sacred, world and church,
*   since it is the world Christ came to and died for.*

A church

without the answers, but asking the right questions;

holding law and grace, freedom and authority, faith and works together in
tension, by the Holy Spirit, pointing to the glorious mystery who is God.

So deeply rooted in gospel and tradition that, like a living tree, it can swing
in the wind and continually surprise us with new blossoms.

Let us dream of a church

with a radically renewed concept and practice of ministry
and a primitive understanding of the ordained offices.

Where there is no clerical status and no class of Christians,
but all together know themselves to be part of the laos—
*   the holy people of God.*

A ministering community
rather than a community gathered around a minister.

Where ordained people, professional or not, employed or not, are present for
the sake of ordering and signing the church's life and mission,
*   not as signs of authority or dependency,*
*   nor of spiritual or intellectual superiority,*

but with Pauline patterns of 'ministry supporting church' instead of the
common pattern of 'church supporting ministry.'

Where bishops are signs and animators of the church's unity, catholicity and
apostolic mission,

priests are signs and animators of her eucharistic life and the sacramental
presence of her Great High Priest,

and deacons are signs and animators—living reminders—of the church's
servanthood as the body of Christ who came as, and is, the servant slave of
all God's beloved children.

PROPHECIES, DREAMS, AND VISIONS

Let us dream of a church

so salty and so yeasty that it really would be missed
 if no longer around;
where there is wild sowing of seeds
 and much rejoicing when they take root,
but little concern for success, comparative statistics, growth or even survival.

A church so evangelical that its worship, its quality of caring, its eagerness
to reach out to those in need cannot be contained.

A church

in which every congregation is in a process of becoming
 free—autonomous—self-reliant—interdependent,

 none has special status:
 the distinction between parish and mission gone.

But each congregation is in mission
and each Christian, gifted for ministry;
 a crew on a freighter, not passengers on a luxury liner.

Peacemakers and healers
 abhorring violence in all forms (maybe even football),
 as concerned with societal healing as with individual healing;
 with justice as with freedom,
prophetically confronting the root causes of social, political and economic ills.

A community: an open, caring, sharing household of faith
 where all find embrace, acceptance and affirmation.

A community: under judgment,
 seeking to live with its own proclamation,
therefore,
 truly loving what the Lord commands
 and desiring His promise.

And finally, let us dream of people called

to recognize all the absurdities in ourselves and in one another,
 including the absurdity that is LOVE,

Do You Believe?

serious about the call and the mission
  but not, very much, about ourselves,
who, in the company of our Clown Redeemer can dance and sing
  and laugh and cry in worship, in ministry and even in conflict.

—*Wesley Frensdorff*[1]

CHAPTER 13

Conclusions and Recommendations

Regarding the old covenant:
> The Lord our God made a covenant with us at Horeb. Not with our ancestors did the Lord make this covenant, but with us, who are all of us here alive today. The Lord spoke with you face to face at the mountain, out of the fire.... And he said: I am the Lord your God ... you shall have no other gods before me. ... for I the Lord your God am a jealous God ... showing steadfast love to the thousandth generation of those who love me and keep my commandments. (Deuteronomy 5:2–4, 5–7, 9b, 10)

Regarding the new covenant:
> As the Father has loved me, so I have loved you; abide in my love.... This is my commandment, that you love one another as I have loved you. ... You are my friends if you do what I command you. I do not call you servants any longer, because the servant does not know what the master is doing; but I have called you friends, because I have made known to you everything that I have heard from my Father. You did not choose me but I chose you. And I appointed you to go and bear fruit, fruit that will last, so that the Father will give you whatever you ask him in my name. I am giving you these commands so that you may love one another. (John 15:9–17)

Since the introduction of the 1979 Book of Common Prayer, the Episcopal Church has had an emphasis on baptismal identity and ministry. I have studied survey responses from forty Episcopal congregations that were recommended as having significant lay development and involvement: where the majority of their members were noticeably and purposefully living into their baptismal commitment to live out the Gospel message in their daily lives. These congregations showed growing awareness that formation in Christian life and ministry could be based primarily and consciously on the covenantal relationship as outlined in the

1979 baptismal ritual. The actual concept of baptismal covenant, while strong in several congregations, is just beginning to catch on, or is not apparent, in others.

Most of the congregations did emphasize fellowship, education, and ritual prayer. Most offered adult education or Bible study and provided some type of opportunity for small group interaction and sharing. Many of the congregations described an open and welcoming attitude, while the importance of the tradition and ritual, as well as being an "Episcopal presence" in the community, were also mentioned. A few congregations had ongoing methods for dealing with conflict resolution or other means to repent and return to the Lord. About half of the congregations were involved in some evangelization efforts and 11 percent indicated that proclaiming the good news of Christ was a priority. Also, *all* of the congregations performed some type of ongoing service, but there was not a consistent understanding that *everyone*, using their Spirit-given gifts, had an important role to play in the Body of Christ. About half of the congregations employed a discernment process. But these processes were sometimes used just to put a church ministry team into place, or as a psychological analysis in order to determine innate talents and abilities for use in the church's own worship or program activities, rather than as gifts from God for support and growth intended for use in all contexts of daily life. A few of the congregations had a priority of promoting justice and peace but many admitted to not being directly involved at all in these areas.

In addition to these findings directly related to the covenantal promises, two other interrelated observations are noteworthy. The first involves the language used by the interviewee in telling me their congregation's story, which reflected the inclination either to speak about God or to refrain from speaking in a faith-based language. The words people use and the stories they tell reflect who they are. According to John Savage, "Everyone tells stories. . . . Hidden inside those stories, like diamonds in the rough, are the deep truths of the unconscious. Storytelling is a form of self-disclosure. You cannot avoid telling your story. You can only try to make it abstract, in an attempt to hide the deeper struggles you are experiencing."[1] This orientation either to use faith-based language or not to use it may be an indicator that points to my second observation: In the church's management of its activities, if emphasis is put mainly on maintaining the organization's existence, the result could be a turning away from God and God's vision in order to buy into the business paradigm. The danger here is that if there is a total reliance on the ways of the world, then this perpetuation of the institution could become idolatry. "Churches will continue to decline, rot, and die if a change in outlook and spirit does not occur. We must not simply tinker with church structures and expect great change [E- to E+]. We cannot simply do the same old things the same old way and expect to get new results. As Christians we must join together in a concerted effort to call the people back to God and to challenge them to grow in their witness and demonstration of God's Word for our time"[2] [M+].

It is therefore interesting to observe that, based on the language that they used during the interview and in their written materials, one half of the congregations evidenced a belief, reliance, and relationship with God, while the other half did not articulate these aspects. Those who did not mention a relationship with God focused instead on themes of survival, ministry and service activities, plans and programs, and community building. Many of the congregations did not have, or did not consistently use, a clear mission or vision statement defining the church's relationship with God and community even though this could help keep the organization and its ministers focused on the things of God rather than on just the priorities of the human institution.

> Then Jesus began to teach them that the Son of Man must undergo great suffering, and be rejected by the elders, the chief priests, and the scribes, and be killed, and after three days rise again. He said all this quite openly. And Peter took him aside and began to rebuke him. But turning and looking at his disciples, he rebuked Peter and said, "Get behind me, Satan! For you are setting your mind not on divine things but on human things."
>
> He called the crowd with his disciples, and said to them, "If any want to become my followers, let them deny themselves and take up their cross and follow me. For those who want to save their life will lose it, and those who lose their life for my sake, and for the sake of the gospel, will save it. For what will it profit them to gain the whole world and forfeit their life? Indeed, what can they give in return for their life? Those who are ashamed of me and of my words in this adulterous and sinful generation, of them the Son of Man will also be ashamed when he comes in the glory of his Father with the holy angels." (Mark 8:31–38)

Understanding the "Focus of Ministry" polarity can help, for a balance in emphasis is needed. The church as a movement, focused on the people's relationship with God, can be harmonized with putting energy into the church as an enterprise, as the institution focuses on organizing the people, and aids the relationship by preservation of the teachings and tradition. The Christian church institution baptizes individuals into the church community with all the rights and privileges and responsibilities appertaining thereto. And the Episcopal baptismal covenant in this context can be marvelously well rounded—introducing people in detail to the mysterious habits of God [M+]—but it can also turn into *pro forma* rites or rigid rules and expectations carved into stone tablets [E-]. Hinsdale compares an active community member's comment—"I have no problem with . . . joining the church. But not if it's to control me. Not if it's to keep me in line. Not to keep a rein on my soul, because my soul is free"—to the local minister's attitude that he doesn't like people saying that they have faith in God and that they will accomplish things with the help of God, when it's not backed up with any exhibition of faith such as belonging to a church.[3] Or, again, in a church that has bought into the business model, such an organization might be tempted to make "baptismal covenant" and "baptismal ministry" into jargon or catch phrases, and using them to establish "benchmarks."[4]

> It is particularly appropriate to note that church size and "success" are of less concern than momentum and faithfulness. For spiritual faithfulness and momentum overcome the fear of chaos that often accompanies such exploration and imagination. In the understanding of truth as resident in our relationship to Jesus Christ, there is the freedom to be who we are, as we are, where we are, and as we are growing to be missioners in Christ, ambassadors for Christ.[5]

For the past twenty-five years the Episcopal Church has had a baptismal ritual that emphatically defines baptism as the initiation of the Christian's life of ministry, and its implications are beginning to take root. The official canons of the church, also, have progressively developed in this area and currently define the importance of all baptized persons by stating:

> Each Diocese shall make provision for the affirmation and development of the ministry of all baptized persons, including: (a) Assistance in understanding that all baptized persons are called to minister in Christ's name, to identify their gifts with the help of the Church and to serve Christ's mission at all times and in all places. (b) Assistance in under-standing that all baptized persons are called to sustain their ministries through commitment to life-long Christian formation.[6]

But the language of *baptism, baptismal covenant*, and *baptismal ministry* is still the language of the institutional church; it is the language of the clergy, not the people. In 1995, Stewart Zabriskie wrote, "Old systems die hard, and we cannot yet claim a total victory. It will take at least another generation for truly shared ministry to become the tradition, for systemic reordering to become a deeply rooted reality, though we are well on our way. Once congregations discover their own gifts for administering a parish and their resources for doing mission work in their own communities, they are unwilling to go back to 'the old ways.' They feel, quite rightly, that they would miss being-and-doing ministry."[7]

Twenty-six of the congregations that I studied were asked specifically about how baptism tied in with lay involvement in their congregations. There was not a clear indication in the responses and the language used by the respondents that the baptismal covenant was the impetus for everyone's actions and decisions in this area. In fact, 20 percent of the congregations had begun their emphasis on lay involvement *prior* to the introduction of the 1979 Book of Common Prayer. Noticeably though, most of the clergy with a seminary education and those locally trained under the old Title III, Canon 9 did use this theological language of baptism. And of the staff who were asked, only one replied that he did not use the terminology of baptismal ministry formally, but the understanding and meaning were there nonetheless. But half of the non-ordained representatives who were asked this question did not use "baptism" as a basis for their understanding of why their members should be involved in God's work. Some sample comments included: "All are invited to the renewal of baptismal covenant during the worship service, but not anything more that I can think of." Another, when asked about their understanding of baptism and whether there was a connection to involvement, responded: "Sort of—I guess—I don't really know. There are a lot of sermons about it. . . ." When asked how her understanding of baptism fit with lay involvement, another responded "What do you mean?" It is interesting to note that the diocesan recommendation for that congregation expressed that the people "have become more excited about and committed to the Ministry of all the Baptized as they have found how important ordained presence is to sustaining the sacramental core and providing a development resource for living into their Baptism." Clearly baptismal ministry is still the language of the church administrators. But 25 percent of the non-ordained representatives *did* use the baptismal covenant language. One member, where the congregation's mission statement was "A Training Center for Daily Ministry," said, "I can't say how baptism fits specifically, but it's there and it got through to me." Another interviewee replied, "Baptism is the beginning of our Christian journey. Baptism gives authority and responsibility to people." The remaining 25 percent of the non-ordained who were questioned, however, spoke in hierarchical terms of "pulling people up for lay leadership."

Figure 13. Language of Baptismal Covenant by Role of Interviewee

	Language of Baptismal Covenant		
	Use baptism language	Don't use	Hierarchical language
Clergy	9	1	
Staff	2	1	
Lay member	2	4	2
Canon 9	5		

Some congregations as a whole did make reference to the people living out their baptismal covenant, but expressed little sense that when utilizing the covenant analogy God is seen as the primary agent, in fact, *initiating the relationship*—"without exception it is God who begins the dialogue."[8] The focus instead was on the people and their gifts rather than on the giver and the overall purpose or mission. There also seemed to be an attempt in some of the congregations to bypass the underlying relationship with God [M] to get to an immediate acceptance and utilization of the talents in order to complete the ordinances mandated by the baptism ritual, or simply to complete the tasks seen as necessary to being a church organization [E].

In light of my research, it would appear that Christians in general do not automatically think back to their baptism, or the promises made in that context, or to baptismal ministry, in order to determine what actions they will take. The questions they grapple with are generally more basic and relational: "What is God calling me to do in this situation (or with my life)?" or "What can I do to make a contribution to the communities I live in?" or just "What can I do to help?" And when God's call to love is carved on the Christian's mind and heart, the language is of service and the response is one of relationship—perhaps less formal, but more intimate than a structured covenant. "No longer shall they teach one another, or say to each other, 'Know the LORD,' for they shall all know me, from the least of them to the greatest," says the LORD (Jeremiah 31:34). But for those who do not yet "Know the Lord" [**M**], the organized Christian community [**E**] is essential: for in sharing faith stories it can be discovered that participating in the initiation ritual of baptism, covenanting with the Lord of the Kingdom, accepting God's help, and developing a relationship leading to a partnership with the Trinity all point in different terminology to the same reality.

The use of language is also important in how people think about themselves and view their roles. A few of the congregations mentioned that using the term *lay person* or *laity* had become awkward. This is not surprising since a lay person is defined in the *negative—not* of a particular profession, or *lacking* extensive knowledge about a subject. The term, because of its connotations, can easily be taken pejoratively, even when it is meant descriptively. Thus, the term *laity* in the context of the church refers to a person's lower status in the church's hierarchical organization, that is, "not clergy," "not a leader in the Christian community." I feel that using the term *lay person* or *laity* falls in the negative quadrant of the Enterprise Focus of Ministry [**E-**] for the term says nothing positive about one's ministry or one's relationship with God [**M+**]. I would recommend that the Episcopal Church consciously choose to change the language and adopt terminology such as *Christian* to describe its members. Other possibilities include *disciple, follower of Jesus, Episcopal Christian,* or even *church member.* Being "Christian" or a "disciple" refers to a broader and more positive reality.[9] To be a "Christian" implies a relationship with Christ [**M+**] and can also be used to denote one's resulting ongoing responsibility to live as Christ lived—beyond church-related activities, at home, at work, in the community, and throughout creation—with the help of God.

In researching this topic I have noticed that many authors have focused on the "lay person's" role in the secular world and in some cases opposite the "clergy" role. Let me cite some examples:

- Kraemer states: "But if the laity of the Church, dispersed in and through the world, are really what they are called to be, the real uninterrupted dialogue between Church and world happens through them. They form the daily repeated projection of the Church into the world. They embody the meeting of Church and World."[10]
- Menking and Wendland advise: "As a layperson, most of your service

will be aimed at promoting the world's good in the settings where you live and work every day."[11]

- Jean M. Haldane states: "Laity, in particular have as their primary arena for ministry the institutions and structures of society in which they work, learn, and play on a daily basis."[12]

- Dozier, too, states: "It is the task of the church, the people of God, to minister within the structures of society. It is the role of the church, the institution, to support that ministry."[13]

But consider also how L. William Countryman describes this tendency to view clergy and laity as *opposites*:

Is the polarity one between church and world, with the priesthood of the laity belonging to the world and the priesthood of the clergy to the church? To put it another way, is secular life the ministry of the laity or does ministry always relate to the church? . . . A definition that treats clergy and laity as polar opposites will never be capable of revealing their mutual interdependence. . . . Without some recognition of our interdependence, laity and clergy will continue to find one another mutually threatening.[14]

As I said above, to be a Christian implies a relationship with Christ and can also be used to denote one's resulting responsibility, beyond church-related activities, to live as Christ lived: at home, at work, in the community, and throughout creation. Thus, instead of concentrating simply on how to make the Christian people aware of their ministry outside of the church, in the secular world of their daily lives, I recommend that the church refocus on God—engendering institutional as well as personal repentance and conversion. The real issue is not one of appropriate roles, but of moving God's love into one's heart and therefore thoroughly into one's mind and thoughts, the whole self or soul. Thus, with the help of God, God's love is demonstrated in all situations and throughout one's life through the gifts given by the Holy Spirit. This is giving oneself totally in loving service to God: not a tithe, nor one or two days a week, not excusing oneself by thinking that it is really impractical to do those things that are preached about in "the real world," but unequivocally. No matter where they are, such Christians will find themselves being sacramental, that is, actively showing God's love which is a true commitment, challenging yet supportive. This will happen at home, work, and, sometimes hardest of all, in the institution called "church." And it is here in the church community where *all* members are to come back together, both bringing support and being supported. It is where they assemble bringing their ministerial selves, their works of service, their Christian witness, their partnership with God. It is this church community where they are to participate fully in the liturgy, which is "the work of the people." Here they will celebrate their communion with God and each other.

Jesus' own baptism by John in the river Jordan symbolizes this covenant between God and humankind. "It was the beginning of Jesus' own ministry, which continues through the covenant community. When Christians accept baptism, they become part of this ministry of Jesus."[15] Because the support of the Christian community [E] is integral to spreading the faith and to its development [M], understanding the dynamics involved in the "Focus of Ministry Polarity" can be of great value. Being aware of these dynamics will make it possible to manage the Focus of Ministry well, through a conscious effort to stay positively balanced without waiting to fall into one of the negative quadrants. And, of course, during a crisis that may bring the congregation impulsively into a negative quadrant, it is beneficial to know the appropriate positive response. By acknowledging Christ [M] as the head [E], the language of the covenant relationship can delineate the balance that allows the management of the polarity in the Christian community's focus for loving service. The Episcopal Church is then free to use whatever is honestly true, noble, right, pure, lovely, admirable, excellent, or praiseworthy in its business practices.

> Let your gentleness be known to everyone. The Lord is near. Do not worry about anything, but in everything by prayer and supplication with thanksgiving let your requests be known to God. And the peace of God, which surpasses all understanding, will guard your hearts and your minds in Christ Jesus. Finally, beloved, whatever is true, whatever is honorable, whatever is just, whatever is pure, whatever is pleasing, what-ever is commendable, if there is any excellence and if there is anything worthy of praise, think about these things. Keep on doing the things that you have learned and received and heard and seen in me, and the God of peace will be with you. (Philippians 4:4–9)

In so doing the church will stay true to God's mercy and love, which is conveyed by the covenantal tradition it chooses to use and which is embraced by its corporate entity: its corporal body.

Joe Vitunic's congregation practices the following as the means to best incorporate its people into the body of Christ:

- Weekly small groups ("Koinonia Groups") that meet in members' homes for Bible study, prayer, and caring for one another
- A philosophy of every-member ministry that is based in the stated purpose of the Church, which includes "equipping every member for ministry"
- A "New Members Class" that everyone is required to take before join-ing the Church and in which both small groups and every-member ministry is stressed
- A weekly roster of Sunday morning ministry assignments that deliberately attempts to involve as many participants as possible

- A ministry strategy that emphasizes a "team" approach and, therefore, maximizes participation
- Periodic teaching on the Holy Spirit and spiritual gifts along with the administration of a spiritual gifts inventory
- A series of courses on relationships that teaches relationship skills and explores self-understanding as well as caring for others and, also, employs much small group work
- Various retreats—men's, women's, healing, Vestry, youth, staff, Alpha—that facilitate building relationships
- The Alpha program that promotes deep fellowship and sharing among the participants and models the working of the body of Christ in small groups and ministry teams.[16]

This list is a good example of how an organized approach [E+] can help a congregation to stay focused on its spiritual purpose and relationship with God [M+]. However, Vitunic goes on to say, "All that said, we do not consider ourselves to have excelled yet in the task of incorporation."[17] Thus the question: "What more could be done?" And perhaps the basic recommendation is not based on which program to offer but accepting an approach of "peace and patience." First and always be at God's service and then be ready for the windows that open when life's turning points or chaotic elements bring opportunities for conversion, recommitment, or deeper intimacy. Because these moments are happening all the time for one person or another, it is important for a congregation to provide *ongoing* means for building a person's relationship with God. Examples of this include personal and authentic prayer (as individuals, in small groups, and as a corporate body), Bible study and reflection on God's message, spiritual direction, spiritual retreats and workshops, and personal support as well as spiritual guidance from the Christian community. Congregations themselves, too, need to be aware of those moments, such as a financial crisis, scandal, or simply the pastor accepting a different call, that are opportunities to be attentive to the Spirit's prompting the corporate body to further growth and spiritual development.

The baptismal covenant is the ritual tradition [E+] embraced by the Episcopal Church to celebrate and renew these moments in which people turn toward God's mercy and love [M+]. God always initiates a loving relationship, but in addition to the ritual of baptism it takes ongoing openness, education, commitment, and personal desire to understand and live fully the covenant in partnership with God. This call and response is not always obvious in the ritual, though; in fact the ritual texts have been adapted and changed through time. Some of the original concepts were emphasized in the tradition while others were abandoned or lost. The 1549 Book of Common Prayer contained instructions to the godparents that definitely reflect the two-sided covenantal agreement:

Well beloved friends, ye have brought these children here to be Baptized,

ye have prayed that our Lord Jesus Christ would vouchsafe to receive
them,
to lay his hands upon them, to bless them, to release them of their sins,
to give them the kingdom of heaven, and everlasting life.
Ye have heard also that our Lord Jesus Christ hath promised in his gospel,
to grant all these things that ye have prayed for:
which promise he for his part, will most surely keep and perform.
Wherefore, after this promise made by Christ,
these infants must also faithfully for their part promise
by you, that be their sureties, that they will forsake the devil and all his
works,
and constantly believe God's holy word,
and obediently keep his commandments.[18]

Although these instructions were kept in the baptism ritual for hundreds of
years, they were omitted when the 1928 version of the Book of Common Prayer
was published. This was not a sudden change; the 1789 Book of Common Prayer
allowed for certain sections to be skipped over with the instruction that "the
intermediate parts of the Service shall be used, once at least in every month, (if
there be a baptism) for the better instructing of the People in the Grounds of Infant
Baptism." In 1979, the baptismal ritual is still referred to as a covenant, but the
emphasis is on the promises made by the newly baptized rather than on the
creation of a partnership or God's initiative.

Some may view the term "covenant" itself as archaic and, in fact, it is. The
tradition of covenant is very rich and calls back to ancient primordial rituals and
relationships that formed not just baptism, but the Eucharistic Communion
sacrament as well. In order to live the baptismal covenant fully, the richness of the
ritual needs to be combined with education and the experience of the living God,
otherwise the words and actions will be without full expression of thought and may
appear meaningless and inert. But whether or not the language of "covenant" is
used, the concept is of a partnership with God—that all of humanity is created for
union with God and in God's image.[19]

Daniel B. Stevick, in the "Supplement to *Prayer Book Studies* 26," which was
the background paper and commentary written in preparation for acceptance of
the 1979 BCP baptismal rite, wrote, "Official liturgical texts in themselves can give
only imperfect direction."[20] But with the help of God, the Episcopal Church and its
people will choose to accept, celebrate, and espouse the relational baptismal
covenant again and again. "Each time this rite of initiation is practiced, the church
is reinstituted and the community renews its covenant to participate in God's
mission for the world."[21] Thus, the church will not lose sight of its stated mission
"to restore all people to unity with God and each other in Christ . . . as it prays and
worships, proclaims the Gospel, and promotes justice, peace, and love . . . through
the ministry of all its members" (BCP, 855).

The First Wave

The green wave
Rose up before me
Blocking the sky.
It broke into white
Expanding fan and cracked,
Undertow pulling my small
Feet out from under me.
I felt my bottom then
Scrape along the rough sand
When my father's giant hand
Reached down to grab my arm
And wrench me out of water
Suddenly to dazzling light,
The ocean pouring off
My shoulders—
Baptism.[22]

Questions for Reflection

1. Do you feel the term *covenant* is a fitting image to use for baptism into the Christian community and for affirming one's relationship with God? Why or why not?

2. Through studying the concepts in this book, have you/your congregation been able to intensify your relationship with God?

ADDITIONAL RESOURCES

Basic Materials

The Art of Teaching the Bible: A Practical Guide for Adults. Christine Eaton Blair. Louisville, KY: Geneva Press, 2001.

Becoming a Blessed Church: Forming a Church of Spiritual Purpose, Presence, and Power. N. Graham Standish. Herndon, VA: The Alban Institute, 2005.

Be Still: Designing and Leading Contemplative Retreats. Jane E. Vennard. Herndon, VA: The Alban Institute, 2000.

The Bible.

The Book of Common Prayer. The Episcopal Church. New York: The Seabury Press, 1979.

Christians at Work: Not Business as Usual. Jan Wood. Scottdale, PA: Herald Press, 1999.

Coalition for Ministry in Daily Life. http://www.dailylifeministry.org.

Discerning Your Congregation's Future: A Strategic and Spiritual Approach. Roy M. Oswald and Robert E. Friedrich, Jr. Herndon, VA: The Alban Institute, 1996.

The Empowering Church: How One Congregation Supports Lay People's Ministries in the World. Davida Foy Crabtree. Herndon, VA: The Alban Institute, 1989.

Episcopal Peace Fellowship, 637 S. Dearborn, Chicago, IL 60605. Phone: 312-922-8628. Email: epfnational@ameritech.net. Website: www.episcopalpeace-fellowship.org.

From Listening Hearts: Discerning Call in Community. Suzanne G. Farnham, Joseph P. Gill, R. Taylor McLean, and Susan M. Ward. Harrisburg, PA: Morehouse Publishing, 1991.

Grounded in God: Listening Hearts Discernment for Group Deliberations. Suzanne G. Farnham, Stephanie A. Hull, and R. Taylor McLean. Harrisburg, PA: Morehouse Publishing, 1999.

In Transition: Navigating Life's Major Changes. W. Wayne Price. Harrisburg, PA: Morehouse Publishing, 2002.

Listening to God: Spiritual Formation in Congregations. John Ackerman. Herndon, VA: The Alban Institute, 2001.

Living on the Border of the Holy: Renewing the Priesthood of All. L. William Countryman. Harrisburg, PA: Morehouse Publishing, 1999.

Marking Time: Christian Rituals for All Our Days. Linda Witte Henke. Harrisburg, PA: Morehouse Publishing, 2001.

Ministry in Daily Life: A Practical Guide for Congregations. William E. Diehl. Herndon, VA: The Alban Institute, 1996.

The Once and Future Church: Reinventing the Congregation for a New Mission Frontier. (Also *Transforming Congregations for the Future* and *Five Challenges for the Once and Future Church.*) Loren B. Mead. Herndon, VA: The Alban Institute, 1991.

Reclaiming the Great Commission: A Practical Model for Transforming

Denominations and Congregations. Claude E. Payne and Hamilton Beazley. San Francisco, CA: Jossey-Bass, 2000.

Small Group Outreach: Turning Groups Inside Out. Jeffrey Arnold. Downers Grove, IL: InterVarsity Press, 1998.

The Soul of Tomorrow's Church: Weaving Spiritual Practices in Ministry Together. Kent Ira Groff. Nashville, TN: Upper Room Books, 2000.

Total Ministry: Reclaiming the Ministry of All God's People. Stewart C. Zariskie. Herndon, VA: The Alban Institute, 1995.

Transforming Church Boards into Communities of Spiritual Leaders. Charles M. Olsen. Herndon, VA: The Alban Institute, 1995.

The Holy Spirit: "I have much more to say to you, more than you can now bear. But when . . . the Spirit of truth comes, [you will be guided] into all truth." (John 16:12–13 NIV)

Additional resources used specifically by the recommended congregations:

Spiritual Growth

Alpha: A program designed for those interested in Christianity. Each session includes a meal, a presentation, and small group discussion. Website: http://alpha-course.org. Email: info@alphacourse.org.

Catechumenate: Preparation for baptism based on early Christian traditions. Includes instruction, opportunities for spiritual growth, and liturgical rites. Website for The North American Association for the Catechumenate: http://www.catechumenate.org. Contact for the Episcopal Church is Clay Morris, Episcopal Church Center, 815 Second Avenue, New York, NY 10017, e-mail: cmorris@episcopalchurch.org.

Centering Prayer: Contemplative prayer whose purpose is to develop the ability to listen and be open to God. Specifically mentioned were Fr. Thomas Keating, as well as the Rev. Sandy Casey-Martus of the Alta Retreat Center, 20 Alta School Rd., Alta WY 83414, website: http://www.altaretreatcenter.org, e-mail: info@altaretreatcenter.org.

Contemplative Prayer: Wordless prayer that focuses on God's goodness and love.

Cursillo/Ultreya: A movement to assist in the development of Christian leaders. It involves a three-day weekend, ongoing supportive groups, occasional large group meetings, and spiritual direction. Website: http://www.episcopalcursillo.org, toll-free phone: 1-877-858-7392.

Faith Alive: An Episcopal program designed to reexamine baptism and confirmation commitments. It takes place over a weekend in the local church buildings as well as small group neighborhood meetings. It is designed to include adults, teens, children, and includes a visit to shut-ins. Faith Alive!, 431 Richmond Place, N.E., Albuquerque, NM 87106, e-mail: FAOfficeNM@aol.com, phone: 505-255-3233.

Inquirers'/Orientation/baptism Classes: Programs designed to provide Christian formation to those interested in joining a church. The sessions are often open to other members who wish to deepen their faith.

Labyrinth: A meditation device that resembles a maze, but has clear unobstructed pathways. Some are large and ornate walkways, while others are simply made from local stones set in order; still others may be designed small enough for tracing with ones finger.

Monastic Spirituality: Structured spiritual exercises to foster the search for God based on traditional practices. Such religious orders often include prayer, silence, fasting, work, study, and good deeds. There are many books on the traditional monastic orders such as the Benedictine, Franciscan, Dominican, and Carmelite practices. Listings and descriptions of current monastic groups can be found on the website of CAROA (Conference of Anglican Religious Orders in the Americas): http://www.orders.anglican.org/caroa and the website for the National Episcopal Church: http://www.episcopalchurch.org/8020_8847_ENG_HTM.htm.

Spiritual Retreats: A withdrawal from everyday life for a time in order to reconnect or connect more fully with God. May be done privately or with a group. Often includes structured activities such as prayer, meditation, study, presentations, and work with a spiritual director. (This type of retreat is not to be confused with working meetings sometimes held off-grounds, often called "staff retreats" or "vestry retreats," in which the focus is on completing an agenda such as the programming for the coming year or setting long-term goals and objectives.)

Taizé Services: Worship based on the style of an international, ecumenical community founded in Taizé, France in 1940 by Brother Roger. The services, which often appeal to young adults, involve a meditative atmosphere and simple repetitive songs, as well as Scripture readings, silence, and intercessory prayers. Their website includes information on music, publications, and how to structure a service: http://www.taize.fr/en.

Church Organization Methods

Comprehensive Database of Congregation Members: Computer programs and staff or members who are computer proficient can be used to track information on members' interests, gifts, employment, and volunteer activities.

Conference Attendance: Attendance and involvement by staff and members at local, regional, and national workshops and conferences can broaden the scope of Christian church and mission past the insular.

Connextions (Formerly Leadership Training Network): "Leadership Connection exists to influence, train, and resource the church to equip people for biblical team ministry, resulting in personal and community transformation" (from their website: http://www.connextion.org). Contact person: Carolyn Cochran, 972-761-0099, PO Box 85094, Richardson, TX 75085, e-mail: carolyncochran@connextion.org.

Ecumenical Partnerships: Working with other Christian churches and organizations for common goals. This can be done one-on-one with neighboring congregations, or on a broader scale. In the United States, you may contact the Office of Ecumenical and Interfaith Relations of the Episcopal Church, USA, 815 Second Avenue, New York, NY 10017, phone: 212-716-6220, e-mail: ecumenical@episcopalchurch.org, or the National Council of Churches, 475 Riverside Drive, Suite 880, New York, NY 10115, website: http://www.ncccusa.org. The worldwide organization is located in Switzerland: World Council of Churches, PO Box 2100, 150 Route de Ferney, CH-1211 Geneva 2, Switzerland, website: http://www.wcc-coe.org.

The Equipping Church: Serving Together to Transform Lives and The Equipping Church Guidebook, by Sue Mallory and Brad Smith (book and workbook), Grand Rapids, MI: Zondervan, 2001. This book is described as a method for organizing the congregation into teams based on their gifts.

Faith Sharing as Part of Vestry Meeting: Is the church about God's business, or just about business? *Transforming Church Boards into Communities of Spiritual Leaders* by Charles M. Olsen (Herndon, VA: The Alban Institute, 1995) addresses this issue.

Leadership Training: Jesus trained his disciples and apostles before he sent them out. In similar ways it is necessary to prepare the members for Christian life and mission. The Bible is the best starting place for this area.

Living Stones: This is a partnership of about twenty Episcopal and Canadian Anglican dioceses that are committed to developing baptismal ministry. Claire Cowden, Diocese of Northwest Texas, 1802 Broadway, Lubbock, TX 79401, phone: 806-763-1370. A spin-off organization is the Ministry Developers' Collaborative, website: http://www.mindevelopers.org. Contact person: Kevin Thew Forrester, e-mail: kevintf@upepiscopal.org.

Mutual/Team/Total Ministry: These are terms often used in association with locally trained clergy and local ministry development. "Team" implies working together for a common goal, "mutual" connotes a shared ministry, and "total" refers to the ministry to which all of the members are called.

Personnel Focused on Members' Development and Gifts: Many congregations found it helpful to have either a paid or unpaid staff person specifically responsible for the ministry development of their members.

"*Purpose Driven Church* in an Episcopal Manner": The Saddleback Church was founded in 1980 by Rick Warren. It now has an attendance of over 20,000. Rick Warren wrote *The Purpose-Driven Church: Growth without Compromising your Message and Mission* in 1995 (Grand Rapids, MI: Zondervan).

Start Up! Start Over!: This is a five-day seminar on congregational development designed for congregation and diocesan teams. It is sponsored by the Episcopal Office of Congregational Development, 815 Second Avenue, New York, NY 10017, website: http://www.episcopalchurch.org/startup.htm. Conference coordinator is Sally O'Brien, phone: 800-334-7626 ext. 6003, e-mail: sobrien@episcopalchurch.org.

Team Work by Congregations, Deaneries, and Dioceses: Many of the smaller congregations reported successful endeavors when they partnered with other churches and made use of their diocesan resources.

Whole Body Ministry: The belief, based on New Testament concepts, in which everyone is connected to God and therefore contributes to the whole.

Christian Formation

Baptismal Covenant Study: An investigation of the depth and meaning behind the vows taken at baptism and renewed in confirmation. See the Book of Common Prayer pages 304–5.

Bible Studies: Sometimes studying the readings one-by-one, based on the upcoming Lectionary readings (http://www.io.com/~kellywp), or by attempting to study the Bible as a whole by using something like the Kerygma program (http://www.kerygma.com).

The Disciple Bible Study: A thirty-six-week Bible study that prepares people to become disciples. Published by Abingdon Press, this series is available through Cokesbury (http://www.cokesbury.com).

Disciples of Christ in Community (DOCC): This program is designed to build community and provide spiritual growth. Training is required for the church team consisting of presenters and group facilitators. Contact Weta Butterfield, phone 800-722-1974, e-mail: docc@sewanee.edu, at the School of Theology Programs Center, University of the South, website: http://www.sewanee.edu/Theology/DOCCFolder/DOCChome.html.

Education for Ministry (EFM): A four-year Episcopal program covering Scriptures studies, church history, liturgy, and theology. University of the South, Sewanee, website: http://www.sewanee.edu/EFM/EFMhome.html. For information e-mail: efm@sewanee.edu, or phone 800-722-1974.

Family Classes and Groups: While some congregations preferred to separate members by age and interest for education and liturgy, others found it beneficial to keep family units together for their growth on the spiritual journey.

The Rev. Michael Merriman: Resource person for the Catechumentate for Baptism and Confirmation. He is currently working at the Episcopal Church of the Transfiguration, 14115 Hillcrest Road, Dallas, TX, 75254.

Outside Speakers: This doesn't have to be a costly endeavor. Sharing and trading experiences of what works and doesn't work with neighboring congregations can make each an "expert" to someone who hasn't tried it at all yet.

Youth Materials: Children's materials can be found at this website: http://www.sermons4kids.com. Materials for youth are available at the following sites: http://www.youthministry.com and http://www.youthspecialties.com.

Fellowship

Book Study Groups: This can work by using either a spiritual selection or by finding spiritual applications in a secular work.

Fellowship Dinners: Much can be said about sharing meals with family, friends, enemies, and church members. It is an opportunity to share life.

Foyer Groups: Implying the welcome and intimacy of a fireplace and hearth, these groups focus on developing relationships rather than on study.

Men's and Women's Groups: These are traditional Episcopal service-oriented groups, such as Episcopal Church Women, but can also be created depending on the needs of the congregation.

Recovery Groups: When the congregation's members are dealing with common issues or traumas, such as grief or illness, it is appropriate and healthy to acknowledge it and offer support and recovery groups, which are often spiritually based, as needed.

Small Groups: Small groups can provide the needed Christian community that isn't attainable by oneself and isn't always easy to find in the larger corporate worship experience. Small groups can be of various types: ranging from support groups, to Bible study, to mothers' groups, to service ministry groups. Even the vestry, altar guild, and other ongoing committees can act like a basic Christian community.

Worship Services

Charismatic Services: Prayer services that recognize the power and presence of the Holy Spirit. Often these services can include lively songs, prayer, praise, speaking in tongues, and prophecy. Contemporary praise music often has a charismatic sense.

Contemporary Services: Services that address persons living in today's world were mentioned as valuable, since participating in such services was more helpful in connecting spiritual church life with day-to-day life in the world.

New Zealand Prayer Book: This book is often used for its ability to draw out the depth of meaning from familiar services by using similar, yet different, words and inclusive language. The original 1989 version is out of print. It is available through the Episcopal Bookstore (http://www.episcopalbookstore.com) in a HarperCollins edition.

1928 Services: Just as some need the connection with modern life in their worship and others need youth services, there are people who are most in tune with God through the worship they may have grown up with. Various previous editions of the Book of Common Prayer are available online at: http://justus.anglican.org/resources/bcp/index.html.

Third-Millennium Services: Recognizing that the Episcopal Church is living into the future, there was a sense by some congregations to use all that is good in the world today in order that all people may worship God fully.

Repentance

Healing Services: Many congregations include a healing rite in the Sunday service or have a separate service regularly. The Book of Common Prayer includes "Ministration to the Sick," pp 453–61, with readings and rites for use on such occasions.

Conflict Management: A suggestion for dealing with conflict came from one congregation who found it quite helpful: *Moving Your Church Through Conflict* by

Speed Leas (Herndon, VA: The Alban Institute, 1985).

Reconciliation Services: Many people don't seem to realize that "confession" is a part of the Episcopal tradition even though many in the church would benefit from each other's forgiveness. Information regarding the ministry of reconciliation can be found in the Book of Common Prayer on page 446. Here it describes that another Christian, as well as a clergyperson, may be asked to hear someone's confession. Two forms for the rite "The Reconciliation of a Penitent," with an absolution by a bishop or priest, are also available on pages 447–52.

Proclamation

Discipleship: Having been made a disciple of Jesus (perhaps through one of the Christian Formation programs described above), it will be natural for one to want to share his or her faith and good news with others.

Urban Theology Unit: Located in Sheffield, England, this organization is said to provide great training materials and resources to engage people in Gospel ministries. Their website is: www.utusheffield.fsnet.co.uk.

Service and Mission

Bridge Builders: This group assists in organizing short-term mission trips in the developing world. Contact Christ Eaton, e-mail: chris@bridgebuilders.org, PO Box 76299, St. Petersburg, FL 33734-6299, phone: 727-551-9060, website: www.bridgebuilders.org.

Commissioning Services: It is appropriate to recognize publicly the gifts given by the Holy Spirit for ministry. The Book of Common Prayer provides a "Celebration of a New Ministry" (BCP, 559–64), which is most often used when installing a priest in a congregation. However this service can also be adapted as needed: "It may also be used for . . . the inauguration of other ministries, diocesan or parochial. . . . Alterations in the service are then made according to circumstances" (BCP, 558).

Local and Global Mission Involvement: Many congregations partner with a sister congregation. One mistake sometimes made is to think that a congregation doesn't have enough money or resources for involvement in mission activities. In reaching beyond oneself, one's experience of God expands. On the other hand, often those who think that they have a lot to give those more needy then themselves find that they received more from their gesture than they gave.

Ministry and Service Groups: Some small groups are formed in order to provide necessary Christian formation. Another activity for small groups to consider is ministry and service. Although there will always be more to learn, it is also necessary to broaden the boundaries of the circle of disciples to reach out to others as well.

Short-Term Mission Activities that Transform Lives: Going outside of one's familiar world and into the world of another child of God can alter your way of thinking about both the other person and yourself. Mission trips don't have to be halfway across the world; often there is mission territory less than halfway across the city.

Peace and Justice

Community Organization Efforts: Ministry in daily life may involve injustices that are occurring on the local level. Sometimes there are interfaith organizations already in place that target such issues that may request the assistance of the local churches. In other instances your congregation may feel called by God to address these issues directly, either through cooperation with other organizations to change the system or by ministry to the victims, or both.

Peace and Justice Groups: Affiliation with local and national groups can help educate the congregation about the various issues. The Episcopal Peace Fellowship is one such networking agency. Their national contact information is Episcopal Peace Fellowship, 637 S. Dearborn, Chicago, IL 60605, phone: 312-922-8628, e-mail: epfnational@ameritech.net, website: http://www.episcopalpeacefellowship.org.

Discernment

Adventure in Awareness: A class originally offered by Margaret Webb and based on the Myers-Briggs Type Indicator. It assists people become aware of their preferences and how they relate to the world around them.

Church Innovations Institute: A research and consulting firm that has been used to help congregations discern roles and attitudes of their members. Website: http://www.churchinnovations.org. Contact info: Church Innovations, 1563 Como Avenue, Suite #103, St. Paul, MN 55105, phone: 888-223-7909, e-mail: information@churchinnovations.org.

Gifts Discernment Workshops/Tools: Devoting specific time, attention, and prayer to the discernment of God's gifts will help give the message that this church community is serious about God's action in each person's life. There are books and other resources available. Go ahead and try it, even if you don't find something that matches your specific circumstances. If you make a mistake, God will let you try it again.

Gifts Discovery Course: "What in God's Name are you doing?" Curriculum developed by St. John's Church, 191 Country Road, Barrington, RI 02806, phone: 401-245-4065, e-mail: stjbar@worldnet.att.net.

Life Cycles: Created by the Episcopal Dioceses of Northern Michigan, Nevada, Wyoming, and in partnership with Leader Resources, this resource has been used to build a community of support for clergy and laity in choosing ministry roles. Their self-description indicates that it "is a process of ongoing spiritual formation within a ministering community. It is a way for adults to explore and deepen their faith, discover and use their gifts for ministry and be transformed by Christ." Website: http://www.leaderresources.org/lifecycles. Contact information: Leader-Resources, 4300 Montgomery Avenue, Suite 104, Bethesda, MD 20814, phone: 800-941-2218.

Myers-Briggs Type Indicator: An inventory that results in one of sixteen personality types. Many sources are available for this assessment. People often believe that knowing their tendencies or preferences will help them better understand themselves, their relationships with others, and their career or ministry options. While, no doubt, this is the case, I am sure that God often calls a person beyond their initial tendencies to further growth as a human being.

SHAPE Discernment Tool: From Saddleback Church, Lake Forest, CA, this instrument profiles a person's spiritual gifts, heart, abilities, personality, and experience, to discern how one can be in ministry with other people. Saddleback follows the profile with a one-on-one talk with a ministry representative in order to connect the person with a Saddleback ministry.

The Three Colors of Ministry: Based on the three dimensions of God's nature, this assessment tool encourages a balanced approach to Christian ministry and service. It is available through ChurchSmart Resources, 3830 Ohio Avenue, Saint Charles, IL 60174, phone: 800-253-4276, e-mail: customerservice@churchsmart. com, website: http://www.churchsmart.com.

Also needed:"Life changing relationship with Christ."

APPENDIX 1

Diocesan Comments Regarding Recommended Congregations

Baptismal Ministry

- Provides in a very conservative community a positive and strong theological, biblical, liturgical, and ecclesial alternative for many people. Hence, its growth both in numbers and Christian formation in the past decade, its outreach and service ministries, its impact and visibility in the community, and its empowerment of baptismal ministries.

- Both congregations have become more excited about and committed to the Ministry of all the Baptized, as they have found how important ordained presence is to sustaining the Sacramental core and providing a development resource for living into their Baptism.

- The parish functions much like a Benedictine House in that there is a high level of interdependence among the congregation that is grounded in their Baptismal ministry.

- This congregation has been working on baptismal ministry development for about four years. They have developed "internal" ministries (preachers, pastoral leaders, priests, deacons), but more significantly, have a clear understanding of ministry "beyond the walls"—at home, on the job, in school, on the soccer field.

Discernment Process

- The Parish Commission on Ministry seeks to meet with individuals who are discerning what their personal everyday ministries may be, as well as shepherding those who are called to ordination or to licensed lay ministries.

- A diocesan leader in gifts identification and ministry development.

Discipleship

- Excellent disciple-making at all ages, involved in mission locally and globally.

Empowering Lay People

- Growing quickly, priest-in-charge has been significant in empowering lay people for ministry-teaching classes, leading small groups, building plans and campaign, networking with other churches.

- This rector gives serious attention to the gifts of lay people and supports lay ministry very effectively.

- I know lay involvement, inclusion of new members and lay-led ministries is [sic] growing. I will let the parish speak for itself.

Evangelism
- Rector has trained lay evangelists.
- They are asking the question, "What does this have to do with our call to bear the Good News to this community?"

Growth
- Both congregations have had substantial increases in Sunday attendance and both are on the road to even greater growth.
- They have remodeled the church, reached out to the community, and most impressive, they have tripled in size.
- Fast-growing mission congregation.
- This may or may not be the place, but is active and one of the fastest growing congregations in the United States.

Lack of Regular Clergy
- For many years this parish had minimal involvement from the clergy. The rectors from 1979 to 2000 were not involved in the day-to-day living of the church. Many teaching, doing, and living projects were begun. . . .
- When a priest leaves a subsidized church we eliminate the subsidy and this has pushed the churches to do unique and wonderful things without the guidance or hindrance of the clergy.
- No paid clergy—congregation owns this model.
- With only irregular visits of clergy, they have developed a dynamic, multi-generational church community and ministry.

None Yet
- Unfortunately we . . . do not have any parishes with significant lay involvement out in the community as a whole. We are working toward this and pray it will begin to happen in four to five years.

Other
- An excellent job of putting into practice "The Purpose Driven Church" in an Episcopal manner.

Outreach
- Medium size, lay-led endowment, active community outreaches, volunteerism at a superb level. Self-starters abound. . . . a heart for the neighborhood homeless, drug recovery, and small impoverished churches nearby . . . joint outreach effort . . .
- Gifts are shared through daily professional lives that impact the larger community. The parish serves to encourage and support many volunteer efforts in the community. It is difficult to think of an agency, service organization, volunteer group that does not include some member or influence from the parish.

Renewal

- Had come to a lull in its life. They attended "Start Up! Start Over!" and revitalized the congregation. They found opportunities where they had thought there were problems.

Small Groups

- Began small groups about eight years ago.
- Has many new lay offices (roles). Has many cell groups. Ongoing formation processes. Phenomenal growth in a negative growth demographic area. Operates "out-of-the-box."

Social Justice

- A history of engagement with racial issues. . . . Extraordinary outreach programming and community leadership both corporately and individually. Very strong campus ministry . . . that engages students in a variety of service projects at or through the parish. First Hispanic ministry in diocese.

Total/Mutual Ministry

- There is a strong commitment to deepening their awareness, understanding and practicing Total Common Ministry and Ministry in Daily Life.
- This cluster has entered into an intentional ministry of empowering all ministry within the Body. They have built upon years of work in "Total Ministry." They are worth a very close look—currently involved in "Living Stones" and extensive training for local ministry development.
- An excellent program of mutual ministry, involving all aspects and persons in the parish. Excellent mission outreach and evangelism.
- Your brief project description fits what we are doing with Total Ministry in our diocese. Total Ministry begins with the understanding that all people are ministers by virtue of their baptism.

APPENDIX 2

Advice Regarding Increased Involvement

God as the Main Focus

- The job of the priest and of the church organization, is to bring people to a life-changing relationship with Christ, to understand what that means, and then to live it out. That's the heart of Christian ministry. That's the priority, all else flows from that.
- Open the Book and pray to hear God's Word.
- Make sure you're listening to the Whole Body Ministry and not just the professionals.
- Commit Ephesians 4 and Matthew 10:4–23 to memory—work it, pray it, teach it, discuss it, then do it some more.
- Focus on Christ, and pray that the Holy Spirit leads the people.

Essential to Being Church

- We just do our thing. We do what we have to do to keep going. There was a rumor that the church was going to close the doors—one little old man held up his key and said, "Not as long as I have a key."
- If the church doesn't involve the people, they're in deep trouble.
- I think the more involvement the healthier you're going to be. I don't see how you can be a Christian church without the people getting involved.

Involvement in the Local Community and Daily Life

- Discover that a lot of what is done outside of the church is ministry. It's great coming to that "aha!" moment. Look at the people's strengths and gifts and start identifying ways that their daily life is called to be ministry.
- Engage the people in the context of the community in which the congregation is located.
- Increased involvement has worked for this small church with limited resources. It has energized it with new life. The thing is not to just keep the doors open until the five old ladies die: Keep the doors open to do God's work in the community.

Roles

- Be actively involved in one's church. It is the way to really claim it as your own.
- Define real, clear opportunities for connections and involvement.
- Wrestle with your clergy intentionally. Ask the tough questions. What is the point of ordained clergy? Look at the boundaries of the leadership role.

- The priest and congregation should make a covenant of expectations.
- Have term limits for catechists and sabbaticals for priests and others as well.
- Engage the people so that they can see that they play a role. This is essential. The real work is done by priests, but the flip side is that we are all priests.

Involvement of Each Person

- Everybody needs to be involved in some way. Recognize that all have gifts in ministry. Clergy should draw the strengths out of the people.
- Empower people—free them up to know what they do matters. Neither education nor ordination is as important as their gifts and passions. There are so many different things to do and everyone's job is important.
- Communications, communications, communications. It is crucial to keep everyone involved in what is going on and know what decisions are made and why.
- Consider the dynamics of couples and families. If one member is a part of the group and the other isn't, how does the congregation help so that they're not isolated? If a couple is in the group, how does it let them be separate individuals? Don't challenge, exclude, or encourage couples, but be aware of problems.
- Find something that everyone can participate in and feel valued, then do it together. This will build bridges.

Empowerment

- Give the people as much opportunity as possible to be doing ministry.
- Growth in spiritually happens when people take on responsibility. They do more and get things done.
- Trust and delegation are very important. Take a risk and trust people.
- Instead of saying "no," say "yes" and then don't micromanage it.
- Accept whatever people can give, whenever they can give. Have a healthy attitude with no judgments.
- Listen to young people; they feel frustrated if no one listens.
- Have a list of needs and have people sign up to develop their strengths. If someone wants to join an activity, they should try it.
- Always have something for a volunteer to do. Don't let anyone stand around.
- Have a time limit on the job. Be specific with what is wanted and what hours they need to be there.
- Support, train, affirm, and stay in touch with the new ministers.
- Say thank you.
- Don't redo what they have done.

- Nurture, develop, and strengthen increased involvement. Do everything to encourage it. Don't say, "You're not to be trusted with the responsibility." Christian leadership and ministry are crucial if the church is to grow. The strength and courage to grow comes from involving all of the people.

Training

- Be intentional. Set a vision of what the people bring. Provide training, planning, preparation, and thought so people don't feel uncomfortable in their new roles.
- Let people know why something needs to be done and why it is important.
- Educate the people to be more welcoming. The Episcopal Church does not have a reputation of acceptance and of opening doors and hearts to all. Evangelism is not a dirty word.
- Address the issues so that those involved know what they're getting into, and the situations that they can get into, as well as the amount of work to be done in the church.
- Attend leadership training and conferences.
- Make a promotional newsletter of people's experience. This provides a witness: This is exciting, energizing, empowering. The people discover things about themselves they didn't know were there.
- Teach and train the people to be ministers doing what they are already committed to.

Variety of Methods

- Each congregation has their own nature and uniqueness.
- Take the time to explore what other congregations are doing and find your own way to become involved in your church and community.
- We did mutual ministry, but other people have to do it their own way and let the rest of it go. It is fun, exciting, and work. It's liberating. You can't go back after doing it. It's powerful. All have a ministry. Each one is doing what they can, and no one has to be the be-all and end-all, because each does the best they can.
- Everyone ought to try it to the extent possible.

Discernment

- Don't build the congregation on one person's personality.
- Don't bury gifts. Help identify, use, and call forth gifts.
- Keep an open mind.
- Instead of looking at where do we want to go, look at who is here, what their gifts are, and how they can use them.
- Be true to people where they are and what's around them; be

opportunistic. Be excited, involved and active. Pay attention. Do it prayerfully.

- Develop a Discernment Committee process.
- The gifts discernment is essential for both the people and the clergy.
- Foster personalities that have a servant heart attitude, those that eat from the tree of life rather than the tree of knowledge. (Some may be capable and gifted but want to control instead of serve.) Those with a servant heart will develop life-giving relationships and communities of faith.

Learning Process
- Remember that it's ongoing. Right now I'm working on encouraging "membership" (belonging to the body) and "stewardship" (taking responsibility for that with which we have been entrusted). We've done quite a bit of work in recent years on servant leadership formation.
- Be ready to deal with the attitude of "We've got our priest, we don't have to do it."
- Look outside the tradition. Look within the tradition where it's really happening. Pray. Be a learner. Find a mentor/coach. Don't try to get everyone, start with healthy people and early adaptors. Plan to stay a long time. Never grow up. Never live into your dream.
- Be aware of the money that is saved by using locally trained ministry teams and clergy and be ready to reprioritize finances and goals.
- Learn it by trying it. JUST DO IT!!
- Persevere. Don't give up. Have faith. It's a journey.
- Pray, search your souls, and don't give up. It takes hard work and sacrifice. All will work out fine in the end.
- Relax into it and let the Spirit move. Breathe deeply, love each other, breathe deeply again. It's going to be a long process. But there are realities that you never dreamed existed. All of the human issues will come up and need to be dealt with and should be. If you're not having a difficult time, you're not doing it right. Truly speak the truth in love to each other, both in times of conflict or struggle, and in times of affirmation. Speak to each other so that you are heard by other parishioners as well.

Ritual
- Lift up and celebrate each ministry on Sundays in the liturgy to show its importance. For every group in the church on a rotating cycle, the members are brought forward, commissioned, prayed over, mentioned in the sermon, and then they host the coffee hour and are available to answer questions and recruit new members.
- Use Pentecost as Baptized Ministry Celebration Sunday.

NOTES

CHAPTER 1

1. The Episcopal Church, *The Book of Common Prayer and Administration of the Sacraments and other Rites and Ceremonies of the Church Together with the Psalter or Psalms of David According to the use of the Episcopal Church* [hereafter referred to as BCP] (New York: The Seabury Press, 1979).

2. Loren Mead, "Lay Ministry Is at a Dead End," *LayNet*, vol. 15, issue 1 (January 2004): 7.

3. Ibid.

4. Loren Mead, letter to the author (New Haven, November 11, 2004).

CHAPTER 2

1. John L. McKenzie, "Aspects of Old Testament Thought," in *The Jerome Biblical Commentary*, vol. 2, *The New Testament and Topical Articles*, eds. Joseph A. Fitzmyer and Raymond E. Brown (Englewood Cliffs, NJ: Prentice-Hall, 1968), 749 [77:79].

2. Steven L. McKenzie, *Covenant, Understanding Biblical Themes* (St. Louis: Chalice Press, 2000), 32.

3. J. McKenzie, 738 [77:11].

4. Ibid., 753 [77:95–96].

5. Verna J. Dozier, *The Dream of God: A Call to Return* (Cambridge, MA: Cowley Publications, 1991), 88.

6. Meredith G. Kline, *By Oath Consigned: A Reinterpretation of the Covenant Signs of Circumcision and Baptism* (Grand Rapids: William B. Eerdmans, 1968), 51–52ff.

7. S. McKenzie, 12.

8. "But Abram said, 'O Lord GOD, what will you give me, for I continue childless, and the one heir of my house is Eliezer of Damascus?' And Abram said, 'You have given me no offspring, and so a slave born in my house is to be my heir'" (Genesis 15:2–3).

9. Here the Greek is actually "slaves" (*doulos*) as it is in John's account of Jesus' washing the disciples' feet (John 13:1–17).

10. John J. Castelot, "Religious Institutions of Israel," in *The Jerome Biblical Commentary*, vol. 2, *The New Testament and Topical Articles*, eds. Joseph A. Fitzmyer and Raymond E. Brown (Englewood Cliffs, NJ: Prentice-Hall, 1968), 725 [76:106].

11. Robert Banks, *Paul's Idea of Community: The Early House Churches in Their Historical Setting* (Grand Rapids: William B. Eerdmans, 1980), 113.

12. See Joseph A. Fitzmyer, "The Letter to the Romans," in *The Jerome Biblical Commentary*, vol. 2, *The New Testament and Topical Articles*, eds. Joseph A. Fitzmyer and Raymond E. Brown (Englewood Cliffs, NJ: Prentice-Hall, 1968), 295 [53:16].

13. "The Acts of Thomas," in *The Apocryphal New Testament*, translation and notes by M. R. James (Oxford: Clarendon Press, 1924), chapter 26; http://www.earlychristianwritings.com/text/actsthomas.html.

14. Cyril of Jerusalem (315–386), Lecture XX, Second Lecture on the Mysteries of Baptism, 2. *A Select Library of the Nicene and Post-Nicene Fathers of the Christian Church*, ed. Philip Shaff, vol. VII, *Cyril of Jerusalem, Gregory Nazianzen* (Grand Rapids: William B. Eerdmans, 1983), 147.

15. John Chrysostom (347–407), Baptismal Homily II.24 in *The Awe Inspiring Rites of Initiation: The Origins of the R.C.I.A., 2nd ed.*, Edward Yarnold (Collegeville, MN: The Liturgical Press, 1994), 160–61.

16. Ibid., II.21, 159, italics original.

17. Cyril of Jerusalem, Mysteries of Baptism, 4, 147–48.

18. Ambrose (340–397), Concerning the Mysteries, 387 CE, 34. *Nicene and Post-Nicene Fathers*, Vol. X, *Ambrose: Select Works and Letters*, 321.

19. Tertullian (145–220), De Corona III, 204 CE. *The Anti-Nicene Fathers: Translations of the Fathers Down to A.D. 325*, eds. Alexander Roberts and James Donaldson, vol. III *Latin Christianity: Its Founder, Tertullian* (Grand Rapids: William B. Eerdmans, 1985), www.ccel.org/fathers2/ANF-03/anf03-10.htm#P1019_415012.

20. Cyril of Jerusalem, Lecture XXI, Third Lecture on the Mysteries on Chrism, 4, 5. *A Select Library of the Nicene and Post-Nicene Fathers*, 150, italics original.

21. Cyril of Jerusalem, Lecture XXIII, Fifth Lecture on the Mysteries on the Sacred Liturgy and Communion, 3. *A Select Library of the Nicene and Post-Nicene Fathers*, 153.

22. Apostolic Constitutions (circa 380), VII, 22. *The Ante-Nicene Fathers*, Vol. VII, *Fathers of the Third and Fourth Centuries: Lactantius, Venantius, Asterius, Victorinus, Dionysius, Apostolic Teachings and Constitutions, Homily, and Liturgies*, www.ccel.org/fathers2/ANF-07/anf07-47.htm#P6620_2278762.

23. L. William Countryman, *Living on the Border of the Holy: Renewing the Priesthood of All* (Harrisburg, PA: Morehouse Publishing, 1999), 103.

24. The concept of "evil" was connected with being "unclean" (*akathartos*); by this change of heart they are now thus cleansed (see Mark 7:1–23, as well as Mark 1:21–28).

25. See "Covenant" in BCP, 846.

26. John E. Huesman, "Exodus," in *The Jerome Biblical Commentary*, vol. 1, *The Old Testament*, ed. Roland E. Murphy (Englewood Cliffs, NJ: Prentice-Hall, 1968), 56 [3:44].

CHAPTER 3

1. Joel M. Charon, *Ten Questions: A Sociological Perspective*, 5th ed. (Belmont, CA: Thomson Wadsworth, 2004), 55–56.

2. Barry Johnson, *Polarity Management: Identifying and Managing Unsolvable Problems* (Amherst, MA: HRD Press, 1992), 92.

3. Roy M. Oswald and Robert E. Friedrich, Jr., *Discerning Your Congregation's Future: A Strategic and Spiritual Approach* (Bethesda, MD: The Alban Institute, 1996), 32.

4. Roy Oswald, Seabury Institute presentation, Evanston, IL, July 2000. Used by permission. A version also appears in Oswald and Friedrich, *Discerning Your Congregation's Future*, 39–42.

5. Oswald and Friedrich, *Discerning Your Congregation's Future*, 41–42.

6. B. Johnson, *Polarity Management*, 92.

7. L. William Countryman, *Living on the Border of the Holy: Renewing the Priesthood of All* (Harrisburg, PA: Morehouse Publishing, 1999), 61–62; "You have heard it said . . . but I tell you" (Matthew 5:17ff).

8. Larry Rasmussen, "Shaping Communities," in *Practicing Our Faith: A Way of Life for Searching People*, ed. Dorothy Bass (San Francisco: Jossey-Bass, 1997), 123.

9. Verna J. Dozier, *The Dream of God: A Call to Return* (Cambridge, MA: Cowley Publications, 1991), 116.

10. Rasmussen, "Shaping Communities," 128.

11. Bruce Gordon, *Protestant History and Identity in Sixteenth-Century Europe*, vol. 1, *The Medieval Inheritance* (Aldershot Hants, England: Scolar Press, 1996), 18–19.

12. John H. Westerhoff, *A People Called Episcopalians: A Brief Introduction to Our Peculiar Way of Life* (Harrisburg, PA: Morehouse Publishing, 1998), 4.

13. Maxwell Johnson, *The Rites of Christian Initiation: Their Evolution and Interpretation* (Collegeville, MN: Liturgical Press, 1999), 266–67; and Robert K. Greenleaf, *Servant Leadership: A Journey into the Nature of Legitimate Power and Greatness* (Mahwah, NJ: Paulist Press, 1983), 81.

14. B. Johnson, *Polarity Management*, 106.

15. Dozier, *The Dream of God*, 120.

16. Ruth A. Meyers, *Continuing the Reformation: Revisioning Baptism in the Episcopal Church* (New York: Church Publishing, 1997), 40–41.

17. John Westerhoff and Caroline Hughes, *Living into Our Baptism: A Guide to Ongoing Congregational and Personal Growth in Christian Faith and Life* (Wichita, KS: St. Mark's Press, 1992), 2.

SECTION TWO

1. The sermon and meditation were written and delivered by the author to St. Stephen's Episcopal Church, Phoenix, AZ, January 16, 2005. Please feel free to use them, adapting for your needs as necessary.

CHAPTER 4

1. Arlin J. Rothauge, *Sizing Up a Congregation for New Member Ministry*, vol. 1, Congregational Vitality Series (New York: The Service, Education & Witness Group of the Domestic & Foreign Missionary Society, 1996), 5.

2. The Episcopal Church, "Title III, Canon 9: Of the Ordination of Local Priests and Deacons," *Constitution & Canons* (New York: Church Publishing Incorporated, 2000), 76. Used by permission.

3. The Episcopal Church, "Title III, Canon 8: Of the Ordination of Priests," *Constitution & Canons* (New York: Church Publishing Incorporated, 2003), 68.

4. Rothauge, *Sizing Up a Congregation*, 5–6. Used by permission.

5. Adele Cerny, St. Thomas Episcopal Church, Canyon City, OR. Telephone interview by author, notes, Glendale, AZ, September 28, 2002. Used by permission.

6. Stewart C. Zabriskie, *Total Ministry: Reclaiming the Ministry of All God's People* (Washington, D.C.: The Alban Institute, 1995), 42–43, emphasis original.

7. Percentages greater than 100 percent are possible since "percent active" was calculated based on average Sunday attendance rather than on congregational membership.

8. Roberta Wexler, St. John's Episcopal Church, Barrington, RI. Telephone interview by author, notes, Glendale, AZ, October 3, 2002. Used by permission.

9. L. William Countryman, *Living on the Border of the Holy: Renewing the Priesthood of All* (Harrisburg, PA: Morehouse Publishing, 1999), 6.

Chapter 5

1. Condensed from "Another Creation Story," Grace St. Paul's Episcopal Church, Tucson, AZ, http://www.grace-stpauls.org/parish.html. Used by permission.

2. Daniel B. Stevick, *Supplement to Prayer Book Studies 26: Holy Baptism Together with a Form for the Affirmation of Baptismal Vows with the Laying-On of Hands by the Bishop also called Confirmation* (New York: Church Hymnal Corporation, 1973), 14–15.

3. Carlyle Fielding Stewart, *The Empowerment Church: Speaking a New Language for Church Growth* (Nashville, TN: Abingdon Press, 2001), 29–30.

4. A. Wayne Schwab, *When the Members Are the Missionaries: An Extraordinary Calling for Ordinary People* (Essex, NY: Mission Press, 2002), 60.

5. See Stewart, *The Empowerment Church*, 34: "Could it be that our middle-class predilections and higher education have prompted us to disdain and negate the fundamental language of our faith so that many of us feel discomfort or shame in invoking the Holy Ghost's presence and power in our lives?"

6. Mary Ann Hinsdale, et al., *It Comes from the People: Community Development and Local Theology* (Philadelphia, PA: Temple University Press, 1995), 1.

7. Mary Beth Rogers, *Cold Anger: A Story of Faith and Power Politics* (Denton: TX: University of North Texas Press, 1990), 49.

8. Ibid., 50.

9. Letty M. Russell, "Authority in Mutual Ministry: Paternalism, Autonomy, Partnership," *Quarterly Review* 6, no. 1 (Spring 1986): 17.

10. Roy M. Oswald and Robert E. Friedrich, Jr., *Discerning Your Congregation's Future: A Strategic and Spiritual Approach* (Bethesda, MD: The Alban Institute, 1996), 114.

11. Stewart C. Zabriskie, *Total Ministry: Reclaiming the Ministry of All God's People* (Washington, D.C.: The Alban Institute, 1995), 10.

12. Michael Chase, St. Stephen's Episcopal Church, Baker, OR. Telephone interview by author, notes, Glendale, AZ, October 19, 2002. Used by permission.

13. Carl Buffington, New Covenant, Winter Springs, FL. Telephone interview by author, notes, Glendale, AZ, October 11, 2002. Used by permission.

14. Robert K. Greenleaf, *Servant Leadership: A Journey into the Nature of Legitimate Power and Greatness* (Mahwah, NJ: Paulist Press, 1983), 245, emphasis original.

15. Stanley J. Menking and Barbara Wendland, *God's Partners: Lay Christians at Work* (Valley Forge, PA: Judson Press, 1993), 14.

16. L. William Countryman, *Living on the Border of the Holy: Renewing the Priesthood of All* (Harrisburg, PA: Morehouse Publishing, 1999), 4–5.

CHAPTER 6

1. Excerpts from Walter M. Miller, Jr.'s *A Canticle for Leibowitz* (New York: Bantam Books, 1959; August 1976 edition), 69, 70–72, 75, 181. Reprinted by permission of Don Congdon Associates, Inc. copyright 1959, renewed 1987 by Walter M. Miller, Jr.

2. Verna J. Dozier, *The Dream of God: A Call to Return* (Cambridge, MA: Cowley Publications, 1991), 6.

3. Carl Buffington, New Covenant, Winter Springs, FL. Telephone interview by author, notes, Glendale, AZ, October 11, 2002. Used by permission.

4. Carlyle Fielding Stewart, *The Empowerment Church: Speaking a New Language for Church Growth* (Nashville, TN: Abingdon Press, 2001), 42–43.

5. David J. Bosch, *Transforming Mission: Paradigm Shifts in Theology of Mission* (Maryknoll, NY: Orbis Books, 1991), 53.

6. Stewart, *The Empowerment Church*, 79–80.

7. Roy M. Oswald and Robert E. Friedrich, Jr., *Discerning Your Congregation's Future: A Strategic and Spiritual Approach* (Bethesda, MD: The Alban Institute, 1996), 12.

8. Verna Dozier and Celia Allison Hahn, *The Authority of the Laity* (Washington, DC: The Alban Institute, 1982), 27.

9. Stewart, *The Empowerment Church*, 78.

10. L. William Countryman, *Living on the Border of the Holy: Renewing the Priesthood of All* (Harrisburg, PA: Morehouse Publishing, 1999), 175.

11. A. Wayne Schwab, *When the Members Are the Missionaries: An Extraordinary Calling for Ordinary People* (Essex, NY: Mission Press, 2002), 180; see also Roy W. Trueblood and Jackie B. Trueblood, *Partners in Ministry: Clergy and Laity* (Nashville, TN: Abingdon Press, 1999), 19.

12. Oswald and Friedrich, *Discerning Your Congregation's Future*, 121.

13. Ibid., 12.

14. Caroline A. Westerhoff, *Calling: A Song for the Baptized* (Boston: Cowley Publications, 1994), 70.

15. Ibid.

16. Schwab, *When the Members Are the Missionaries*, 119.

17. Stewart, *The Empowerment Church*, 75–76.

18. Oswald and Friedrich, *Discerning Your Congregation's Future*, 121, 117, 118.

19. Dozier, *The Dream of God*, 27.

20. "Catechumenate," *The Book of Occasional Services 1991* (New York: The Church Hymnal Corporation, 1991), 125.

CHAPTER 7

1. Bobbi Wexler, St. John's Episcopal Church, Barrington, RI. Letter to the author, October 18, 2004. Used by permission.

2. Roland Allen, *The Spontaneous Expansion of the Church: The Causes that Hinder It* (London: World Dominion Press, 1956), 122.

3. A. Wayne Schwab, *When the Members Are the Missionaries: An Extraordinary Calling for Ordinary People* (Essex, NY: Mission Press, 2002), 165–67. See also Mary Ann Hinsdale, et al., *It Comes from the People: Community Development and Local Theology* (Philadelphia, PA: Temple University Press, 1995), 202.

4. Stewart C. Zabriskie, *Total Ministry: Reclaiming the Ministry of All God's People* (Washington, D.C.: The Alban Institute, 1995), 63; Carlyle Fielding Stewart, *The Empowerment Church: Speaking a New Language for Church Growth* (Nashville: Abingdon Press, 2001), 56.

5. L. William Countryman, *Living on the Border of the Holy: Renewing the Priesthood of All* (Harrisburg, PA: Morehouse Publishing, 1999), 11–12, emphasis original.

6. Robert Banks, *Paul's Idea of Community: The Early House Churches in Their Historical Setting* (Grand Rapids: William B. Eerdmans, 1980), 111–12, emphasis original.

7. Leonardo Boff, *Ecclesiogenesis: The Base Communities Reinvent the Church* (Maryknoll, NY: Orbis Books, 1986), 71; Caroline A. Westerhoff, *Calling: A Song for the Baptized* (Boston: Cowley Publications, 1994), 67; Schwab, *When the Members Are the Missionaries*, 111, 116; Patricia N. Page, *All God's People are Ministers: Equipping Church Members for Ministry* (Minneapolis, MN: Augsburg, 1993), 19–20; 84–85; and Caroline Westerhoff, *Calling*, 51.

8. Phyllis Snyder, St. John's Episcopal Church, Marietta, PA. Telephone interview by author, notes, Glendale, AZ, September 26, 2002. Used by permission.

9. Beth Ely, St. Philip's Episcopal Church, Greenville, SC. Telephone interview by author, notes, Glendale, AZ, October 10, 2002. Used by permission.

10. Diane Adams, diocesan recommendation letter, dated June 10, 2002. Used by permission.

11. Page, *All God's People are Ministers*, 86.

12. Countryman, *Living on the Border of the Holy*, 12–13.

13. Roy M. Oswald, *Making Your Church More Inviting: A Step-by-Step Guide for In-Church Training* (Bethesda, MD: The Alban Institute, 1992), 49–50.

14. Countryman, *Living on the Border of the Holy*, 5–6.

15. M. Shawn Copeland, "Saying Yes and Saying No," in *Practicing Our Faith: A Way of Life for Searching People*, ed. Dorothy Bass (San Francisco: Jossey-Bass, 1997), 68.

16. Roy M. Oswald and Robert E. Friedrich, Jr., *Discerning Your Congregation's Future: A Strategic and Spiritual Approach* (Bethesda, MD: The Alban Institute, 1996), 146.

17. Verna J. Dozier, *The Dream of God: A Call to Return* (Cambridge, MA: Cowley Publications, 1991), 149–50.

18. "From the beginning, at the healthy center of this process has been a commitment to the spirituality of the parish vocation; they have had regular parish and

vestry retreats—actually going away to reflect on their life together and where they are being led. *I suspect this accounts for the energy level in the parish and the attraction it holds for newcomers"* (Zabriskie, *Total Ministry*, 56, emphasis added; see also Galatians 5:22–25).

Chapter 8

1. St. Martin's-in-the-Field Episcopal Church, Severna Park, MD, "Connect?" and "Commit?" adult education brochures, October 2004 and January 2005. Used by permission.

2. Verna J. Dozier, *The Dream of God: A Call to Return* (Cambridge, MA: Cowley Publications, 1991), 30.

3. Ruth A. Meyers, *Continuing the Reformation: Revisioning Baptism in the Episcopal Church* (New York: Church Publishing, 1997), 205–6.

4. Patricia N. Page, *All God's People Are Ministers: Equipping Church Members for Ministry* (Minneapolis, MN: Augsburg, 1993), 65; Stanley J. Menking and Barbara Wendland, *God's Partners: Lay Christians at Work* (Valley Forge, PA: Judson Press, 1993), 86.

5. Menking and Wendland, *God's Partners*, 30; see also Carlyle Fielding Stewart, *The Empowerment Church: Speaking a New Language for Church Growth* (Nashville, TN: Abingdon Press, 2001), 38–39.

6. Roy M. Oswald and Robert E. Friedrich, Jr., *Discerning Your Congregation's Future: A Strategic and Spiritual Approach* (Bethesda, MD: The Alban Institute, 1996), xi; Eddy Hall and Gary Morsch, *The Lay Ministry Revolution* (Grand Rapids, MI: Baker Books, 1995), 69.

7. Stewart, *The Empowerment Church*, 44; also 45–46; and see also Oswald and Friedrich, *Discerning Your Congregation's Future*, 76.

8. Roland Allen, *The Spontaneous Expansion of the Church: The Causes that Hinder It* (London: World Dominion Press, 1956), 133; see also Stewart, *The Empowerment Church*, 93; and A. Wayne Schwab, *When the Members Are the Missionaries: An Extraordinary Calling for Ordinary People* (Essex, NY: Mission Press, 2002), 99.

9. Schwab, *When the Members Are the Missionaries*, 316; see also Oswald and Friedrich, *Discerning Your Congregation's Future*, 66–67; and Celia Allison Hahn, *Growing in Authority: Relinquishing Control: A New Approach to Faithful Leadership* (Washington, DC: The Alban Institute, 1994), 149.

10. Frank Rogers, Jr., "Discernment," in *Practicing Our Faith: A Way of Life for Searching People*, ed. Dorothy Bass (San Francisco: Jossey-Bass, 1997), 115; see also Hahn, *Growing in Authority*, 168, 169–170, 179.

11. Oswald and Friedrich, *Discerning Your Congregation's Future*, 42.

12. Dozier, *The Dream of God*, 3.

13. See Schwab, *When the Members Are the Missionaries*, 109.

14. See Oswald and Friedrich, *Discerning Your Congregation's Future*, 42.

15. Oswald and Friedrich, *Discerning Your Congregation's Future*, 18; see also Larry Rusmussen, "Shaping Communities," in *Practicing Our Faith: A Way of Life for*

Searching People, ed. Dorothy Bass (San Francisco: Jossey-Bass, 1997), 120.

16. Page, *All God's People Are Ministers*, 53.

17. Caroline A. Westerhoff, *Calling: A Song for the Baptized* (Boston: Cowley Publications, 1994), 141.

18. Victor Horvath, Immanuel, Bellows Falls, VT. Telephone interview by author, notes, Glendale, AZ, September 30, 2002. Used by permission.

CHAPTER 9

1. Adapted from Priscilla King, "Immanuel—'God with us,'" *Immanuel's Good News* (Bellows Falls, VT: Immanuel Episcopal Church, July and August 1999), 4.

2. A. Wayne Schwab and Willian A. Yon, "Faith and Gospel in My Life," in *Ministry in Daily Life: A Guide to Living the Baptismal Covenant*, eds. Linda L. Grenz and J. Fletcher Lowe, Jr. (New York: Episcopal Church Center, 1996), 46.

3. L. William Countryman, *Living on the Border of the Holy: Renewing the Priesthood of All* (Harrisburg, PA: Morehouse Publishing, 1999), 76.

4. Michael Chase, St. Stephen's Episcopal Church, Baker, OR. Telephone interview by author, notes, Glendale, AZ, October 19, 2002. Used by permission.

5. Stanley J. Menking and Barbara Wendland, *God's Partners: Lay Christians at Work* (Valley Forge, PA: Judson Press, 1993), 86.

6. Richard R. Broholm, "Toward Claiming and Identifying our Ministry in the Workplace," in *Ministry in Daily Life: A Guide to Living the Baptismal Covenant*, eds. Linda L. Grenz and J. Fletcher Lowe, Jr. (New York: Episcopal Church Center, 1996), 92.

7. John Westerhoff and Caroline Hughes, *Living into Our Baptism: A Guide to Ongoing Congregational and Personal Growth in Christian Faith and Life* (Kansas: St. Mark's Press, 1992), 23.

8. Roland Allen, *The Spontaneous Expansion of the Church: The Causes That Hinder It* (London: World Dominion Press, 1956), 124.

9. Carlyle Fielding Stewart, *The Empowerment Church: Speaking a New Language for Church Growth* (Nashville, TN: Abingdon Press, 2001), 98.

10. Allen, *The Spontaneous Expansion of the Church*, 13–14.

11. A. Wayne Schwab, *When the Members Are the Missionaries: An Extraordinary Calling for Ordinary People* (Essex, NY: Mission Press, 2002), 108–9.

12. Stewart C. Zabriskie, *Total Ministry: Reclaiming the Ministry of All God's People* (Washington, DC: The Alban Institute, 1995), xiii.

13. Allen, *The Spontaneous Expansion of the Church*, 14.

14. Mary Ann Hinsdale, et al., *It Comes from the People: Community Development and Local Theology* (Philadelphia, PA: Temple University Press, 1995), 203.

15. Eddy Hall and Gary Morsch, *The Lay Ministry Revolution* (Grand Rapids, MI: Baker Books, 1995), 44.

16. Allen, *The Spontaneous Expansion of the Church*, 183-190.

17. Zabriskie, *Total Ministry*, 71.

18. Harriette Burkhalter, Spirit of the Heartland Episcopal Churches, Central Minnesota. Telephone interview by author, notes, Glendale, AZ, October 3, 2002. Used by permission.

CHAPTER 10

1. Article submitted to the author, The Episcopal Church of the Transfiguration, Dallas, TX, January 17, 2005. Used by permission.

2. Caroline A. Westerhoff, *Calling: A Song for the Baptized* (Boston: Cowley Publications, 1994), 32–33.

3. L. William Countryman, *Living on the Border of the Holy: Renewing the Priesthood of All* (Harrisburg, PA: Morehouse Publishing, 1999), 69.

4. Richard R. Broholm, "Toward Claiming and Identifying our Ministry in the Workplace," in *Ministry in Daily Life: A Guide to Living the Baptismal Covenant*, eds. Linda L. Grenz and J. Fletcher Lowe, Jr. (New York: Episcopal Church Center, 1996), 92.

5. Countryman, *Living on the Border of the Holy*, 17–18. See also Roland Allen, *The Spontaneous Expansion of the Church: The Causes that Hinder It* (London: World Dominion Press, 1956), 46; and Robert K. Greenleaf, *Servant Leadership: A Journey into the Nature of Legitimate Power and Greatness* (Mahwah, NJ: Paulist Press, 1983), 13–14.

6. Stanley J. Menking and Barbara Wendland, *God's Partners: Lay Christians at Work* (Valley Forge, PA: Judson Press, 1993), 50–51.

7. Ellen Dingwall, The Episcopal Church of the Transfiguration, Dallas, TX. Telephone interview by author, notes, Glendale, AZ, October 3, 2002. Used by permission.

8. Countryman, *Living on the Border of the Holy*, 30.

9. Stewart C. Zabriskie, *Total Ministry: Reclaiming the Ministry of All God's People* (Washington, DC: The Alban Institute, 1995), 9–10.

10. Roy M. Oswald and Robert E. Friedrich, Jr., *Discerning Your Congregation's Future: A Strategic and Spiritual Approach* (Bethesda, MD: The Alban Institute, 1996), 15.

11. Victor Horvath, Immanuel, Bellows Falls, VT, Parish description brochure. See also Eddy Hall and Gary Morsch, *The Lay Ministry Revolution* (Grand Rapids, MI: Baker Books, 1995), 55; and Patricia N. Page, *All God's People Are Ministers: Equipping Church Members for Ministry* (Minneapolis, MN: Augsburg, 1993), 13.

12. Countryman, *Living on the Border of the Holy*, 169.

13. Michael Chase, St. Stephen's Episcopal Church, Baker City, OR. Letter to author, November 24, 2004. Used by permission.

14. Ibid.

15. The Episcopal Church, "Title III, Canon 9: Of the Ordination of Local Priests and Deacons," *Constitution & Canons* (New York: Church Publishing Incorporated, 2000), 76ff. Used by permission.

16. "No paid clergy—congregation owns this model" (diocesan recommendation letter). Used by permission.

17. Hall and Morsch, *The Lay Ministry Revolution*, 64.

18. St. Martin's-in-the-Field, Severna Park, MD, "Ministry Discernment Workshops" web page, http://www.stmartinsinthefield.com/html/mdw.shtm, accessed October 19, 2002. Used by permission.

19. See also Frank Rogers, Jr., "Discernment," in *Practicing Our Faith: A Way of Life for Searching People*, ed. Dorothy Bass (San Francisco: Jossey-Bass, 1997), 106.

20. Diocesan recommendation letter. Used by permission.

21. Menking and Wendland, *God's Partners*, 100–101.

22. Hall and Morsch, *The Lay Ministry Revolution*, 66; Countryman, *Living on the Border of the Holy*, 142; and Margaret Crane, Immanuel Episcopal Church, Bellows Falls, VT, "Canon Pastor," *Immanuel's Good News* (September and October 1998): 1.

23. Page, *All God's People Are Ministers*, 46.

24. Oswald and Friedrich, *Discerning Your Congregation's Future*, xvii.

25. Zabriskie, *Total Ministry*, 7.

26. Victor Horvath, Immanuel, Bellows Falls, VT. Telephone interview by author, notes, Glendale, AZ, September 30, 2002. Used by permission.

27. Jim Scheible, St. Matthew's Episcopal Church, Chatfield, MN. E-mail interview by author, Glendale, AZ, November 7, 2002. Used by permission.

28. Hall and Morsch, *The Lay Ministry Revolution*, 65.

29. Celia Allison Hahn, *Growing in Authority: Relinquishing Control: A New Approach to Faithful Leadership* (Washington, DC: The Alban Institute, 1994), 159.

30. Stephen M. Kelsey, "Ministry of Discipleship?" in *Ministry in Daily Life: A Guide to Living the Baptismal Covenant*, eds. Linda L. Grenz and J. Fletcher Lowe, Jr. (New York: Episcopal Church Center, 1996), 113.

31. Page, *All God's People Are Ministers*, 86.

32. Oswald and Friedrich, *Discerning Your Congregation's Future*, 78. Zabriskie, *Total Ministry*, 55.

33. Oswald and Friedrich, *Discerning Your Congregation's Future*, 60.

34. Nels Moller, Trinity Memorial Episcopal Church, Rupert, ID. Telephone interview by author, notes, Glendale, AZ, October 4, 2002. Used by permission.

35. David J. Bosch, *Transforming Mission: Paradigm Shifts in Theology of Mission* (Maryknoll, NY: Orbis Books, 1991), 472.

36. Robert Tate, St. Martin-in-the-Field Episcopal Church, Philadelphia, PA. E-mail interview by author, notes, Glendale, AZ, November 1, 2002. Used by permission.

37. Frank Rogers, Jr., "Discernment," 117–18.

38. Oswald and Friedrich, *Discerning Your Congregation's Future*, 9–10.

39. Ibid., ix.

40. Victor Horvath, Immanuel Episcopal Church, Bellows Falls, VT, "Mapmakers," *Immanuel's Good News* (July and August 1997): 1.

Chapter 11

1. Episcopal General Convention Resolution 1988–C030. Used by permission.

2. Episcopal General Convention Resolution 2003–A130. Used by permission.

3. Episcopal General Convention Resolution 2000–D022. Used by permission.

4. Episcopal General Convention Resolution 1976–A069. Used by permission.

5. Episcopal General Convention Resolution 2000–D015. Used by permission.

6. Episcopal General Convention Resolution 2000–A047. Used by permission.

7. Episcopal General Convention Resolution 2003–D006. Used by permission.

8. Mary Ann Hinsdale, et al., *It Comes from the People: Community Development and Local Theology* (Philadelphia, PA: Temple University Press, 1995), 204.

9. Robert Banks, *Paul's Idea of Community: The Early House Churches in Their Historical Setting* (Grand Rapids: William B. Eerdmans, 1980), 118, 121, emphasis original.

10. Eddy Hall and Gary Morsch, *The Lay Ministry Revolution* (Grand Rapids: Baker Books, 1995), 29.

11. L. William Countryman, *Living on the Border of the Holy: Renewing the Priesthood of All* (Harrisburg, PA: Morehouse Publishing, 1999), 188.

12. Hinsdale, *It Comes from the People*, 1, 323.

13. Ibid., 301.

14. Episcopal General Convention Resolutions: 1988–C030, 1994–D124, 1997–A036, 1997–A042, 2000–D015, 2000–D022, and 2000–D052. The complete resolutions are available online at http://www.episcopalchurch.org/ 21867_11723_ENG _HTM.htm. Used by permission.

15. Richard R. Broholm, "Toward Claiming and Identifying our Ministry in the Workplace," in *Ministry in Daily Life: A Guide to Living the Baptismal Covenant*, eds. Linda L. Grenz and J. Fletcher Lowe, Jr. (New York: Episcopal Church Center, 1996), 94–95; and A. Wayne Schwab, *When the Members Are the Missionaries: An Extraordinary Calling for Ordinary People* (Essex, NY: Mission Press, 2002), 107.

16. William Droel and Gregory Augustine Pierce, *Confident and Competent: A Challenge for the Lay Church* (Chicago: ACTA Publications, 1987), 64.

17. Robert K. Greenleaf, *Servant Leadership: A Journey Into the Nature of Legitimate Power and Greatness* (Mahwah, NJ: Paulist Press, 1983), 239–40, emphasis original. See also Verna J. Dozier, *The Dream of God: A Call to Return* (Cambridge, MA: Cowley Publications, 1991), 6, 9; Verna Dozier and James Adams, *Sisters and Brothers: Reclaiming A Biblical Idea of Community* (Boston: Cowley Publications, 1993), 93–94; and Caroline A. Westerhoff, *Calling: A Song for the Baptized* (Boston: Cowley Publications, 1994), 27–28.

18. Schwab, *When the Members Are the Missionaries*, 133–34, 181.

Chapter 12

1. Nan Cobbey, "They Call it 'The Miracle Church'. Congregations Cross Boundaries to Join 'Church' Raising,'" *Episcopal Life* (http://www.episcopal-life.org/26769_ 55294_ENG_HTM.htm, February 1, 2004). Reprinted with permission.

2. Celia Allison Hahn, *Growing in Authority: Relinquishing Control: A New Approach to Faithful Leadership* (Washington, DC: The Alban Institute, 1994), 17.

3. John Westerhoff and Caroline Hughes, *Living into Our Baptism: A Guide to Ongoing Congregational and Personal Growth in Christian Faith and Life* (Kansas: St. Mark's Press, 1992), 91–92.

4. Robert Banks, *Paul's Idea of Community: The Early House Churches in Their Historical Setting* (Grand Rapids: William B. Eerdmans, 1980), 54, emphasis in original; Galatians 4:1ff; Ephesians 4:13ff.

5. M. Scott Peck, *The Road Less Traveled: A New Psychology of Love, Traditional Values and Spiritual Growth* (New York: Simon & Schuster, 1978), 301.

6. Hendrik Kraemer, *A Theology of the Laity* (Philadelphia: Westminster Press, 1958), 147, footnote 2, emphasis added.

7. Westerhoff and Hughes, *Living into Our Baptism*, 30. See also God's assistance to the prophets: Exodus 3:12; Ezekiel 1:3; Daniel 1:17; and Jeremiah 1:7–8.

8. Roy M. Oswald and Robert E. Friedrich, Jr., *Discerning Your Congregation's Future: A Strategic and Spiritual Approach* (Bethesda, MD: The Alban Institute, 1996), 7; Stewart C. Zabriskie, *Total Ministry: Reclaiming the Ministry of All God's People* (Washington, DC: The Alban Institute, 1995), 62.

9. Stanley J. Menking and Barbara Wendland, *God's Partners: Lay Christians at Work* (Valley Forge, PA: Judson Press, 1993), 2; see also page 6; and 98–99.

10. *The Alternative Service Book 1980: Services Authorized for Use in the Church of England in Conjunction with the Book of Common Prayer* (Cambridge, UK: Cambridge University Press, 1980), 247, italics original.

SECTION THREE

1. Charles R. Wilson, "The Dream: Wesley Frensdorff," in *Reshaping Ministry: Essays in Memory of Wesley Frensdorff*, eds. Josephine Borgeson and Lynne Wilson (Arvada, CO: Jethro Publications, 1990), 1–6. Reprinted with permission from the editors.

CHAPTER 13

1. John Savage, *Listening & Caring Skills: A Guide for Groups and Leaders* (Nashville: Abingdon Press, 1996), 77.

2. Carlyle Fielding Stewart, *The Empowerment Church: Speaking a New Language for Church Growth* (Nashville: Abingdon Press, 2001), 107. See also Stanley J. Menking and Barbara Wendland, *God's Partners: Lay Christians at Work* (Valley Forge, PA: Judson Press, 1993), 73–74; and Roland Allen, *The Spontaneous Expansion of the Church: The Causes that Hinder It* (London: World Dominion Press, 1956), 127–28.

3. Mary Ann Hinsdale, et al., *It Comes from the People: Community Development and Local Theology* (Philadelphia: Temple University Press, 1995), 313, 314.

4. A. Wayne Schwab, *When the Members Are the Missionaries: An Extraordinary Calling for Ordinary People* (Essex, NY: Mission Press, 2002), 182.

5. Stewart C. Zabriskie, *Total Ministry: Reclaiming the Ministry of All God's People* (Washington, DC: The Alban Institute, 1995), 88–89.

6. The Episcopal Church, "Title III: Ministry, Canon 1: Of the Ministry of All Baptized Persons, Section 1," *Constitution & Canons*, 2003, 59. Used by permission.

7. Zabriskie, *Total Ministry*, 28. See also M. Scott Peck, *The Road Less Traveled: A New Psychology of Love, Traditional Values and Spiritual Growth* (New York: Simon & Schuster, 1978), 193–94, 266; and Celia Allison Hahn, *Growing in Authority: Relinquishing Control: A New Approach to Faithful Leadership* (Washington, DC: The Alban Institute, 1994), 155.

8. Kevin L. Thew Forrester, "Mutual Ministry & Leadership," unpublished manuscript, 2002, 73.

9. Stephen M. Kelsey, "Ministry or Discipleship?" in *Ministry in Daily Life: A Guide to Living the Baptismal Covenant*, eds. Linda L. Grenz and J. Fletcher Lowe, Jr. (New York: Episcopal Church Center, 1996), 114.

10. Hendrik Kraemer, *A Theology of the Laity* (Philadelphia: Westminster Press, 1958), 169–70.

11. Menking and Wendland, *God's Partners*, 112.

12. Jean M. Haldane, "What Builds the Laity for Ministry?" in *Ministry in Daily Life: A Guide to Living the Baptismal Covenant*, eds. Linda L. Grenz and J. Fletcher Lowe, Jr. (New York: Episcopal Church Center, 1996), 11.

13. Verna J. Dozier, *The Dream of God: A Call to Return* (Cambridge, MA: Cowley Publications, 1991), 142.

14. L. William Countryman, *Living on the Border of the Holy: Renewing the Priesthood of All* (Harrisburg, PA: Morehouse Publishing, 1999), 128.

15. Patricia N. Page, *All God's People Are Ministers: Equipping Church Members for Ministry* (Minneapolis: Augsburg, 1993), 15.

16. Joe Vitunic, Church of the Savior, Ambridge, PA. E-mail to Karen Alger included as part of diocesan recommendation, May 23, 2002. Used by permission.

17. Ibid.

18. From the baptism ritual of the 1549 Book of Common Prayer, http://justus.anglican.org/resources/bcp/1549/Baptism_1549.htm.

19. Ambrose, *Concerning the Mysteries*, 1:2; Cyril of Jerusalem, *First Lecture on the Mysteries*, 1. Gregory Nazianzen, *The Oration on Holy Baptism*, I. Acts 19:1–7, " . . . We have not even heard that there is a Holy Spirit. . . . A treatise on this matter [baptism] will not be superfluous; instructing not only such as are just becoming formed, but them who, content with having simply believed, without full examination of the grounds of the traditions, carry, through ignorance, an untried though probable faith" (Tertullian, *On Baptism*, I).

20. Daniel B. Stevick, *Supplement to Prayer Book Studies 26: Holy Baptism Together with A Form for the Affirmation of Baptismal Vows with the Laying-On of Hands by the Bishop also Called Confirmation* (New York: Church Hymnal Corporation, 1973), 85.

21. Page, *All God's People Are Ministers*, 16–17.

22. Reprinted, by permission, from author Bettie Anne Doebler, *Nine Waves: Poems by Bettie Anne Doebler, Ralph Slotten, Jon Thiem*, ed. Jon Thiem (Lititz, PA: Sutter House, 2003), 29.

REFERENCE LIST

Allen, Roland. *The Spontaneous Expansion of the Church: The Causes that Hinder It.* London: World Dominion Press, 1956.

Banks, Robert. *Paul's Idea of Community: The Early House Churches in Their Historical Setting.* Grand Rapids, MI: William B. Eerdmans , 1980.

Bass, Dorothy, ed. *Practicing Our Faith: A Way of Life for Searching People.* San Francisco: Jossey-Bass, 1997.

Boff, Leonardo. *Ecclesiogenesis: The Base Communities Reinvent the Church.* Maryknoll, NY: Orbis, 1986.

Borgeson, Josephine, and Lynne Wilson, eds. *Reshaping Ministry: Essays in Memory of Wesley Frensdorff.* Arvada, CO: Jethro Publications, 1990.

Bosch, David J. *Transforming Mission: Paradigm Shifts in Theology of Mission.* Maryknoll, NY: Orbis, 1991.

Castelot, John J. "Religious Institutions of Israel," in *The Jerome Biblical Commentary*, vol. 2, *The New Testament and Topical Articles*, eds. Joseph A. Fitzmyer and Raymond E. Brown. Englewood Cliffs, NJ: Prentice-Hall, 1968.

Charon, Joel M. *Ten Questions: A Sociological Perspective.* 5th ed. Belmont, CA: Thomson Wadsworth, 2004.

Church of England, The. *The Alternative Service Book 1980: Services Authorized for Use in the Church of England in Conjunction with the Book of Common Prayer.* Cambridge, UK: Cambridge University Press, 1980.

Cobbey, Nan. "They Call it 'The Miracle Church.' Congregations Cross Boundaries to Join 'Church-Raising.'" In *Episcopal Life* (February 1, 2004) http://www.episcopal-life.org/26769_55294_ENG_HTM.htm.

Countryman, L. William. *Living on the Border of the Holy: Renewing the Priesthood of All.* Harrisburg, PA: Morehouse Publishing, 1999.

Crane, Margaret. "Canon Pastor," in *Immanuel's Good News.* Bellows Falls, VT: Immanuel Episcopal Church (September and October 1998): 1.

Daloz, Laurent A. Parks, et al. *Common Fire: Leading Lives of Commitment in a Complex World.* Boston: Beacon Press, 1996.

Dozier, Verna J. *The Calling of the Laity.* New York: Alban Institute, 1988.

———. *The Dream of God: A Call to Return.* Cambridge, MA: Cowley, 1991.

Dozier, Verna, and James Adams. *Sisters and Brothers: Reclaiming a Biblical Idea of Community.* Boston: Cowley Publications, 1993.

Dozier, Verna, and Celia Allison Hahn. *The Authority of the Laity.* Washington, DC: Alban Institute, 1982.

Droel, William, and Gregory Augustine Pierce. *Confident and Competent: A Challenge for the Lay Church.* Chicago: ACTA Publications, 1987.

Episcopal Church, The. *The Book of Common Prayer and Administration of the Sacraments and Other Rites and Ceremonies of the Church, Together with the Psalter or Psalms of David, According to the Use of the Episcopal Church.* New York: The

Seabury Press, 1979.

———. *The Book of Occasional Services 1991.* New York: The Church Hymnal Corporation, 1991.

———. *Constitution & Canons, Together with the Rules of Order for the Government of the Protestant Episcopal Church in the United States of America Otherwise Known as the Episcopal Church.* New York: Church Publishing Incorporated, 2003.

———. "Title III, Canon 9: Of the Ordination of Local Priests and Deacons." In *Constitution & Canons, Together with the Rules of Order for the Government of the Protestant Episcopal Church in the United States of America Otherwise Known as the Episcopal Church.* New York: Church Publishing Incorporated, 2000.

Fitzmyer, Joseph A. "The Letter to the Romans," in *The Jerome Biblical Commentary,* vol. 2, *The New Testament and Topical Articles,* eds. Joseph A. Fitzmyer and Raymond E. Brown. Englewood Cliffs, NJ: Prentice-Hall, 1968.

Forrester, Kevin Thew. *Leadership and Ministry with a Community of Equals.* San Jose, CA: Inter Cultural Ministry Development, 1997.

———. "Mutual Ministry & Leadership." Unpublished manuscript, 2002.

Gordon, Bruce. *Protestant History and Identity in Sixteenth-Century Europe,* vol. 1, *The Medieval Inheritance.* Aldershot Hants, England: Scolar Press, 1996.

Grace St. Paul's Episcopal Church. "Another Creation Story." Tucson, AZ, http://www.grace-stpauls.org/parish.html.

Greenleaf, Robert K. *Servant Leadership: A Journey into the Nature of Legitimate Power and Greatness.* Mahwah, NJ: Paulist Press, 1983.

Grenz, Linda L., and J. Fletcher Lowe, Jr., eds. *Ministry in Daily Life: A Guide to Living the Baptismal Covenant.* New York: Episcopal Church Center, 1996.

Hahn, Celia Allison. *Growing in Authority: Relinquishing Control: A New Approach to Faithful Leadership.* Washington, DC: The Alban Institute, 1994.

Hall, Eddy, and Gary Morsch. *The Lay Ministry Revolution.* Grand Rapids, MI: Baker Books, 1995.

Hinsdale, Mary Ann, et al. *It Comes from the People: Community Development and Local Theology.* Philadelphia, PA: Temple University Press, 1995.

Horvath, Victor. "Mapmakers," in *Immanuel's Good News.* Bellows Falls, VT: Immanuel Episcopal Church (July and August 1997): 1.

Huesman, John E. "Exodus." In *The Jerome Biblical Commentary,* vol. 1, *The Old Testament,* ed. Roland E. Murphy. Englewood Cliffs, NJ: Prentice-Hall, 1968.

Johnson, Barry. *Polarity Management: Identifying and Managing Unsolvable Problems.* Amherst, MA: HRD Press, 1992.

Johnson, Maxwell E. *The Rites of Christian Initiation: Their Evolution and Interpretation.* Harrisburg, PA: Morehouse Publishing, 1998.

King, Priscilla. "Immanuel—'God with us.'" *Immanuel's Good News.* Bellows Falls, VT: Immanuel Episcopal Church (July and August 1999).

Kline, Meredith L. *By Oath Consigned: A Reinterpretation of the Covenant Signs of Circumcision and Baptism.* Grand Rapids, MI: William B. Eerdmans, 1968.

Kraemer, Hendrik. *A Theology of the Laity.* Philadelphia: Westminster Press, 1958.

McKenzie, John L. "Aspects of Old Testament Thought." In *The Jerome Biblical Commentary*, vol. 2, *The New Testament and Topical Articles*, eds. Joseph A. Fitzmyer and Raymond E. Brown. Englewood Cliffs, NJ: Prentice-Hall, 1968.

McKenzie, Steven L. *Covenant*, Understanding Biblical Themes. St. Louis, MO: Chalice Press, 2000.

Mead, Loren. "Lay Ministry is at a Dead End." *LayNet* (January 2004): 7.

Menking, Stanley J., and Barbara Wendland. *God's Partners: Lay Christians at Work*. Valley Forge, PA: Judson Press, 1993.

Meyers, Ruth A. *Continuing the Reformation: Revisioning Baptism in the Episcopal Church*. New York: Church Publishing Incorporated, 1997.

Oswald, Roy M. *Making Your Church More Inviting: A Step-by-Step Guide for In-Church Training*. Bethesda, MD: The Alban Institute, 1992.

Oswald, Roy M., and Robert E. Friedrich, Jr. *Discerning Your Congregation's Future: A Strategic and Spiritual Approach*. Bethesda, MD: The Alban Institute, 1996.

Page, Patricia N. *All God's People Are Ministers: Equipping Church Members for Ministry*. Minneapolis: Augsburg, 1993.

Peck, M. Scott. *The Road Less Traveled: A New Psychology of Love, Traditional Values and Spiritual Growth*. New York: Simon & Schuster, 1978.

Roberts, Alexander, and James Donaldson, eds. *The Ante-Nicene Fathers: Translations of the Writings of the Fathers Down to A.D. 325*. Grand Rapids, MI: William B. Eerdmans, 1985.

Rogers, Mary Beth. *Cold Anger: A Story of Faith and Power Politics*. Denton, TX: University of North Texas Press, 1990.

Rothauge, Arlin J. *Sizing Up a Congregation for New Member Ministry*, vol. 1, Congregational Vitality Series. New York: The Service, Education & Witness Group of The Domestic & Foreign Missionary Society, 1996.

Rowthorn, Anne W. *Liberation of the Laity*. Wilton, CT: Morehouse Publishing, 1986.

Russell, Letty M. "Authority in Mutual Ministry: Paternalism, Autonomy, Partnership." *Quarterly Review* 6 No 1 (Spring 1986): 10–23.

Schaff, Philip, ed. *A Select Library of the Nicene and Post-Nicene Fathers of the Christian Church*. Grand Rapids, MI: William B. Eerdmans, 1983.

Schaff, Philip, and Henry Wace, eds. *A Select Library of the Nicene and Post-Nicene Fathers of the Christian Church: Second Series*. Grand Rapids, MI: William B. Eerdmans, 1982.

St. Martin-in-the-Field Episcopal Church, Sevena Park, MD, website, http://www.stmartinsinthefield.com/html/mdw.shtm. Accessed October 19, 2002.

Savage, John. *Listening and Caring Skills: A Guide for Groups and Leaders*. Nashville: Abingdon Press, 1996.

Schwab, A. Wayne. *When the Members Are the Missionaries: An Extraordinary Calling for Ordinary People*. Essex, NY: Member Mission Press, 2002.

Stevick, Daniel B. *Supplement to Prayer Book Studies 26: Holy Baptism Together with A Form for the Affirmation of Baptismal Vows with the Laying-On of Hands by the Bishop also called Confirmation.* New York: Church Hymnal Corporation, 1973.

Stewart III, Carlyle Fielding. *The Empowerment Church: Speaking a New Language for Church Growth.* Nashville: Abingdon Press, 2001.

Thomsett, Fredrica Harris. *We Are Theologians: Strengthening the People of the Episcopal Church.* Cambridge, MA: Cowley Publications, 1989.

Trueblood, Roy W., and Jackie B. Trueblood. *Partners in Ministry: Clergy and Laity.* Nashville: Abingdon Press, 1999.

Westerhoff, Caroline A. *Calling: A Song for the Baptized.* Boston: Cowley Publications, 1994.

Westerhoff, John, and Caroline Hughes. *Living into Our Baptism: A Guide to Ongoing Congregational and Personal Growth in Christian Faith and Life.* Wichita, KS: St. Mark's Press, 1992.

Westerhoff, John. *A People Called Episcopalians: A Brief Introduction to Our Peculiar Way of Life.* Harrisburg, PA: Morehouse Publishing, 1998.

Wylie-Kellermann, Jeanie, ed. "Alternative Ways of Doing Church: Looking for Full Participation." *Witness* 77 (August–September 1994): 5–20, 30–31.

Yarnold, Edward. *The Awe-Inspiring Rites of Initiation: The Origins of the R.C.I.A.,* 2nd edition. Collegeville, MN: The Liturgical Press, 1994.

Zabriskie, Stewart C. *Total Ministry: Reclaiming the Ministry of All God's People.* Washington, DC: The Alban Institute, 1995.

PERMISSIONS

Every effort has been made to trace the copyright owners of material included in this book. The author and publishers would be grateful if any omissions or inaccuracies in these acknowledgments could be brought to their attention for correction in any future edition. They are grateful to the following copyright holders: